BRIGHT BLUE BEADS

BRIGHT
BLUE BEADS

An American Family in Persia

By

MAXINE ADAMS MILLER

DRAWINGS BY
R. A. HAYRAPETIAN
TEHRAN, IRAN

THE CAXTON PRINTERS, LTD.
CALDWELL, IDAHO
1965

First printing, May, 1961
Second printing, July, 1961
Third printing, January, 1962
Fourth printing, January, 1965

Library of Congress Catalog Card No. 61-9316

Printed and bound in the United States of America by
The CAXTON PRINTERS, Ltd.
Caldwell, Idaho
97597

To
Sherman, Marlene, Lloyd, and Javad

CONTENTS

ILLUSTRATIONS

BRIGHT BLUE BEADS

I DINED ON YELLOW ROSES

"ROSES! BEAUTIFUL YELLOW ROSES! AND FRAGRANT
—*so* fragrant. Ali, thank you." Inhaling the perfume
I put the gift of roses beside me on the Persian rug.

My husband Sherman, our Persian friend Ali, and I
were having a picnic in the heart of the Kurdish tribal
country. We had just come down a precipitous pass
into a lush valley; farther down the valley snuggled
the town of Sanindaj. We could see it there, all tan
mud walls and houses, no other color, just tan against
the green hills. Sanindaj looked as if it had been slum-
bering for five thousand years. We should speak softly,
I felt—we shouldn't be the ones to awaken it.

On our way from Tehran we had seen men plowing
with the wooden plows of the Bible, Kurdish women
cleaning wool for spinning by beating it with heavy
sticks in a stream, and villagers harvesting wheat with
hand sickles.

May, Sherm decided as we traveled, was definitely
the time to make the trip. Wild flowers were in bloom,
the crops were green, the land beautiful.

"These Kurds are so colorful! I'm so excited about
them," I told Ali.

"You've said that about all the tribes," Ali remarked.
"When we were with the Qashqa'i you thought they

were the most colorful, and the same thing with the Turkomen, Bakhtiari—all the rest."

"I guess so. They're all so gay in their individual ways. Being here in this mail-order brown skirt and blouse makes me feel mighty drab."

In our two years in Iran we had traveled from one end of that fabled land to the other and had been delighted with the hospitality of the villagers, the city dwellers, the tribes and their chiefs. Now we were on our way to Sanindaj, where we would be guests of one of the leading Kurdish khans, or landowners.

We had been officially warned: "You must not be on the road after five o'clock in the afternoon. There are occasional lawless bandits who come down from their mountain hideouts looking for prey. Remember, the Kurds are particularly restless at this time because of Russian propaganda and the tension on the Iraq border. Keep your special permits and border passes where you can get to them at all times."

Through no fault of our own, Ali and Sherm actually had to push me in the stalled *moosh* ("mouse," that's what we called Ali's Volkswagen) the last few miles from Tehran to Kermanshah. We arrived in Kermanshah around midnight. Much of the way there were no real roads, not even ruts. That was difficult enough, but the temperamental *moosh* developed engine trouble.

"When you said nothing but a jeep or a Volks would make it you were right, Ali," said Sherm, "but even the *moosh* almost let you down."

"I hope the khan has someone who can fix it. I am

Kurdish Tribesman

not going to push it all the way back to Tehran. Of course you haven't had *your* turn at pushing," Ali teased me.

Ali rarely traveled without a servant, to help in such emergencies and to prepare tea and picnic lunches. This time Sherm and I had vetoed any extra passengers—it was crowded for three, even. Now we felt guilty.

While poor Ali had stayed with the car, supervising the mechanic for two days in Hamadan, Sherm and I lived it up. We relaxed in the gardens of the lovely Bu-Ali Hotel, peered into shop windows displaying the famous Hamadan blue ware, watched the rug weavers and leather workers, and enjoyed this, another of Persia's prehistoric sites. Hamadan is an ancient city waiting to be discovered by the archaeologists.

We started on our way. The car clunked out again. The men decided to push on, literally, to Sanindaj.

Ali jumped up from our picnic and rolled up the rugs. "The khan will be waiting!" he said. "Better go."

The first two servants stationed at the entrance to the khan's driveway alerted those farther up the line. When we reached the gate it was already open. The khan rushed from the forecourt to greet us. He bowed low, kissed Ali on the cheeks, then had a servant usher us into a living room.

The khan's wife appeared. After greeting us warmly, she immediately engaged Ali in deep conversation. A Kurd, she also spoke Persian fluently.

During our stay she read pages of and quoted from poetry she had written. Translating the fine shadings of Persian into English is difficult but Ali tried.

This woman was dedicated to improving the status of women in her land. She overflowed with ideas on that subject and on the problems of the unfortunates of the country. I was amazed to find a woman who had never been out of Iran, and living in this isolated tribal region, bursting with such plans, such ideas. Furthermore, her husband was backing her on everything.

Servants came and went with tray after tray of food. Then the faithful were called to prayers from the roof of a nearby building. Afterward, tea was served, again, and before we realized it the afternoon had stretched into night.

One servant had stood at attention the entire time. "Ali," I asked, "what is that servant supposed to do?"

"He is the khan's tailor. He is waiting for the word to take you and Sherm to the bazaar. There you will choose the materials for your Kurdish outfits."

It was two days before the khan gave the signal! So far as I could tell the tailor didn't move a muscle all that time.

The hospitality had been overwhelming, a servant always at our elbow to jump at our every whim. When it seemed there was absolutely nothing more that could be offered in the way of food at the welcoming dinner, two servants appeared bearing trays heaped with something that looked like a pudding.

Conversation stopped. Everyone showed great interest in the new dish. One of the servants came to me, first. I took a serving but I had to ask Ali, "What is this?"

"You are lucky. A great delicacy, this. Yellow roses

pudding. From roses just like the ones I picked along the way. Smell!"

"Do you mean it's flavored with yellow roses?"

"Not just flavored. The petals are cooked, then mixed with a little flour, sugar, perhaps something else. And we shall dine again on roses at my farewell party for you."

Suddenly, after all our absorbing months in Persia, talking, traveling, seeing, eating, playing, working, studying, I felt again the sensation of entering a strange, vivid, delicate land, as if I had just then touched down in the home of the khan. The two years in Persia dropped away. I was a girl from Glendale lifting a magic spoonful of rose petals to my lips.

We are back in Glendale now, Sherm and I. There is magic, not to mention convenience, in our American kitchen, but for the taste of yellow roses, altogether Persian, at once real and exotic, we rely on our memories.

Persia was once a never-never land. Now it will never be very far away from us, or our children. In this new kind of world, no matter how removed in time and space and culture, the Glendales and the Sanindajis are not that far apart.

How far? Well, not *that* far! I know this now, but no busy Glendale wife could have felt less prepared than I did when a telephone call jerked my family up by the roots and whirled us off to, of all places, Iran.

I have an uneasy feeling that history is catching up with old Persia all too fast. While Persia's past still lies in plain sight, where an American family could live in it, I'm eager to tell our story. If for no other reason than for myself, to keep the memory of it as fresh as those new roses, as real as those tan mud walls.

CHANGE OF PACE

THE COURSE OF OUR LIVES WAS FOLLOWING THE CHAR-
acteristic pattern for an American professor—Sherman,
me—the professor's wife—and our two, typical teen-
agers—Marlene, fifteen, and Lloyd, eighteen. We are
the kind who plan from the cradle to the grave. Before the children were born we had completed building our home in Glendale, California, and expected to
live in it, without interruption, the rest of our lives.
That is—until the telephone rang.

Dr. Wright, of the University of Southern California,
was on. He told Sherm that "they" wanted him to
set up a School of Business Administration at the University of Tehran, Iran. In addition to that he would
be expected to confer with and advise the businessmen, find out their needs, and help work out their
problems.

"Oh, dear, it's too much trouble to make such a
drastic change when we are all as happy as we are
here," I said. "Our roots are deep and, you know, we
aren't the type who like to be uprooted."

Then I began thinking of all the obstacles between
Glendale and Tehran. Sherm would have to get a
leave of absence from Glendale College, then be cleared
through all sorts of agencies. The children would, no

doubt, resist leaving their friends and plans. We would have to find a caretaker for our house. This was only the beginning. It exhausted me just thinking about it.

However, within the next few days things happened in rapid sequence. After a reading marathon about Iran, we convinced ourselves it would be a great experience. "We will have a trip around the world and, definitely, a change of pace," Sherm said.

On a July morning we climbed into a friend's car with our luggage heaped all around us, in every possible crevice, under our feet and on our laps, and headed for the airport.

After five weeks of absorbing adventures and misadventures through Japan, Hong Kong, Thailand, up and down India, we arrived at Karachi, Pakistan, for our last big push to Tehran.

Here Lloyd was dramatically and suddenly seized with the most serious kind of dysentery. We knew there was an American army hospital in Tehran and since he did not respond to any medication, the doctor in Karachi advised us to get him to Iran as quickly as possible.

Sherm was elected by Marlene and me (Sherm not having a vote) to sit with Lloyd on the plane and play nurse. I can never remember five hours being so interminable.

The loud-speaker announced we were flying over Tehran. I looked down and there it was, set in a granite-hard landscape that seemed to stretch to infinity. The sun was rising and shimmering over the snowy top of Mount Demevend, Iran's highest peak. The setting could have been Salt Lake City with overtones of Palm Springs, California. The rugged Elburz Mountains and the sweep of desert were just as I had imagined they would be.

The "fasten seat belt" sign flashed on. I glued my eyes to the window as we made a perfect landing at Mehrabad airport that last day of August, 1957.

The "grand entrance" which we had all secretly imagined fell *very* short of being grand. However, we felt lucky that we could sneak in ahead of schedule. In our wrinkled, weakened condition, we would have made a frightening impression.

Lloyd could hold up his own head now, and sit half-way up on a hard bench in the airport.

When Sherm got his turn at the customs desk there was much commotion. The clerks walked away and left him standing there, after relieving him of his pass-ports. I knew something was wrong. Perhaps our papers for Iran were not in order. As I was visualizing the prospects of our spending hours, maybe even days there with our sick offspring slowly wasting away, someone shouted, "Meester Meeler, you are ahead of time. Thees is a meestake. You must come thees afternoon."

"That's right, but we are here now." They were shaking hands warmly. "Sorry, but there was a mistake on reservations. Can you help me out? They took my passports and nothing has happened since," Sherm appealed.

"Yes, yes, indeed. I represent the American Embassy. They recognized your name and know you are ex-pected thees afternoon. Thees creates problem."

"What difference does it make to the customs when I arrive?" Sherm inquired.

"Just, just—that eet ees deefferent. You were to come thees afternoon. No worry. All taken care of. You no need to go through more customs." He disappeared and returned shortly with our passports. He signaled to porters to take our luggage. "Follow me," he announced. That's what we did—followed him outside. We spied an airport bus just ready to leave for Tehran. I began to sprint toward it.

"No, no, no—I have sent for private car for you. She coming right away to take you to hotel."

Lloyd was tottering back and forth, leaning on the fence. He spotted the one bench outside of the station proper and immediately fell onto it. We were assured again and again by Mr. Esfanderi that it would only be a few more minutes before our car would arrive. There was no place for the rest of us to sit; we stood on one foot, then the other. Our car arrived in an hour and forty minutes.

When we did get to the hotel they did not have the reservations for which we asked. They had only one very old room. We took it gladly, and found the desk clerk had not exaggerated one bit about its age.

Lloyd dropped into the bed nearest the entrance. While we were searching for a basin in which to wash our hands, the telephone rang. Sherm answered. A friendly conversation ensued, then he hung up.

"The welcoming committee is in the lobby. Word gets around in a hurry. Esfanderi has alerted Bill Morgan, the Director of the Institute for Administrative Affairs."

Marlene wailed, "You will have to go down without me and make excuses. I couldn't possibly go down in this wrinkled old dress."

"Stop complaining, all of you. Wash your dirty faces, comb your hair, and look the best you can. I'll go down right now and try to pave the way for the rest of you liabilities." He stalked out of the room, combing his hair on the way.

Quickly, Marlene and I got ourselves together the best we could, told Lloyd to lie quietly, and marched forth to meet various charming and delightful people who were to become our close and admired friends.

Bill Morgan was a tall, handsome, personable man who immediately inspired confidence. His wife was charming and friendly, and they knew exactly what to do with people in our benumbed and confused state. They had been in Tehran for four years and were old hands at picking up the disorganized pieces of humanity who came to the city to advise the Iranians on how to get organized.

Already they had a suite of rooms for us at another hotel. We moved within the hour and found ourselves very cozily situated.

Lloyd was now able to keep down some broth, so we felt his recovery was ultimately assured. He was most content to lie motionless in bed and alone while we went to the luncheon and dinner.

We were taken to the Morgans' home in Shimran. It fitted the description I had passed on to the family as to what we could expect in housing. The compound gate opened onto an attractive Persian garden and an inviting, glistening swimming pool. The house was typical Tehran, two story, of yellowish-brown brick, with spacious high-ceilinged rooms and lots of them.

One of the leading industries of this city is brick making. The kilns dot the very southernmost section so thickly they give the impression of a forest of factories.

"Boy, wouldn't it be neat if we could find a brick house like this?" Marlene beamed and chirped as we took a tour.

After a refreshing swim, we got our second wind. As we climbed the steps to our rooms, Marlene said, "If today is a sample of the people and fun we are going to have here, I am going to love it." It was, and she did love it—so much so she didn't want to leave—ever.

FRIDAY IS SUNDAY

TOMORROW AND ITS FRENZIED ACTIVITIES CAME. LLOYD was given further treatment at the American Army Hospital and his excellent response to the medication indicated that he would be with us a little longer.

Marlene had to be at the Community School to take an entrance examination at eight in the morning. This is the only high school in Tehran where classes are taught in English. Failing to gain entrance would mean there would be no school for her to attend. It is an American Christian school, organized years ago, primarily for foreigners in Iran and English-speaking Iranians. It's a missionary school and over thirty nations, all the world's great religions, and many cultures are represented here. The Iranian schools are separate—one for boys and one for girls—but Community is co-educational. Here great tolerance for the ideals of others has to be developed.

The school is crowded because of the influx of Americans under Point Four, private business, Army, and State Department. When it was established, naturally, the present-day American influx could not be visualized. Much last-minute planning has been necessary to accommodate even a few of the American students who have applied.

I accompanied Marlene to the examination. Our hotel manager carefully explained to the driver of our rented car how to get there. In all the time I lived in Tehran, I was never able to find it by myself. For a while I thought we would not find it now, or the hotel ever again. The driver would throw up his hands and rant in Persian, not a word of which we understood (but we could imagine what he was saying). He drove wildly around as if he were trying to get out of a maze in a fun house. By some miracle we finally made it. Although late, Marlene was allowed to take the examinations.

On this haphazard jaunt the street scenes of Tehran unfolded before us. We wended our way through one narrow, twisting, unasphalted *kutche* (small street) after another. At this time little did I dream I was to live on one which was much more of an obstacle course than any of these. Some were only wide enough for one car to go through, and full of unbelievable hazards. (Before I left, these same *kutches* began to look quite excellent as compared with others we were to travel.)

Businessmen in natty, pin-striped suits strolled along bareheaded, idly swinging and fingering their *tizbahs* (strings of amber or mother-of-pearl beads). Originally, these were prayer beads, and still are for the deeply religious and the mullahs (religious teachers or Moslem priests). Now they are more popularly used as worry beads instead of fingernail biting, gestures, hair twisting, watch-chain twirling, and other nervous habits. Personally I think the beads are a great substitute and had planned to invest in a string immediately. I was quite let down when I learned that they were used only by the men. Occasionally the beads are employed in making a vital decision, just as we might toss a coin.

The un-Westernized women (older upper class and most all of the lower classes) were wearing the *chador*, the long shrouding capes which completely enveloped them from top to toe. They were in plain black or navy or black background with small white print. This, I discovered, was big-city sophistication, because the farther out of Tehran one goes, the more colorful the *chador*. In the villages several miles out, they became a riot of color.

"Look, Mother, just look at—well—what are they, men?" Marlene pointed at something.

I looked to see ragged men bent over, dozing in the sun, pulling carts or just plodding along. They wore little, round, brown skullcaps; some wore men's striped pajama bottoms for pants. These seemed the most popular apparel among the workmen and serve their purpose well. They are rolled above the knees for working in mud, near water, and on buildings, then covered with their regular crazy-patched pants after work. The over pants are removed and they are ready for sleeping. Very practical.

Outside, hawkers were standing over their pails of fruits, vegetables, and flowers. The tiny shops, not much larger than a good-sized doghouse, displayed their disordered ware through small windows. They reminded me of some of the stores still in our back country where everything from horseshoes to red flannels is sold. In the meat shops, whole lambs and steers, just killed, swayed from the ceilings. Lamb is the meat of the country. The fat-tailed sheep is unique to Iran. The sheep store huge amounts of fat in their tails, from which they live in winter, and when they are killed, this fat is used for cooking. They are a comical sight waddling along, wagging their big fat tails behind them. It's especially ludicrous to see a white one with a henna tail. Pig in any form is forbidden to Moslems, but it can be found in the Armenian meat shops.

Plaintive chants of the street vendors peddling their wares filled the air. When I first heard them I thought they were a call to prayer as the lilting intonations sounded similar to me.

"Everything is so bustling. It must be like a graveyard when everything is closed on Fridays. You know, the Morgans said that is the only day everything folds," Marlene remarked.

"That's right. Friday is Sunday here."

"Going to be odd to have Friday for the sabbath. They said that I will be out of school on Friday, back Saturday, then because it is a Christian school I am out Sunday again. Going to be different, isn't it?" Marlene said.

"You are lucky. The Iranian students only have Friday off and go the other six days a week."

"Yes, but they get two and one-half hours off for lunch every day. Imagine! They go home and take a nap. Most Iranians take a rest in the afternoon, Mrs. Morgan said."

"I know. The stores are closed every day from one until about four. I'll have to get used to that. May even develop the nap habit myself."

"Mrs. Morgan said the worst days to shop are Friday, Saturday, and Sunday. All Moslem stores close Friday, Jewish shops Saturday, and Sunday all the Christians. You better shop the other days, so there will be more stores open," Marlene advised.

Just then four donkeys, sagging under unwieldy loads, appeared from nowhere in front of us. Their driver lazily wandered along unperturbed as the car all but removed his mount's rear.

"Did you see those bright blue beads around those donkeys' necks? Look quick and you can see." Marlene was urgent.

I turned suddenly and got a glimpse of shimmering blue.

"Say, I know what they are for—to ward off the evil eye. That's what someone told me yesterday. Better get some for myself. I'll need a lot of luck today," said my nervous Marlene.

Goats sallied in and out between cars in the next dingy *kutche* and our driver barely missed one, then another, as we slid from side to side on the seat. Flocks of well-disciplined turkeys marched in front of their herder through the thickest of traffic without so much as a flutter of a single wing.

"Doesn't it just kill you—all these walls so we can't see what's behind them? Makes everything look exactly the same. How do people ever find which wall is theirs?" Marlene chattered on, trying her best to di-

vert my mind from the worry of not
we might end our journey. "If a fell
drunk he would never be able to find
his."

"I notice all the homes are behind
shops are out on the streets," I said. "I'
ous to see what's behind them, too. This
here is the old one of Tehran and they s
the important families have lived, an
wealthiest also have homes in Shimra
Tehran, in the summer."

"That's where we are going to live, i
"I hope so—if we can find a suitable
"Look at that fellow! What is he
head?" Marlene was hanging out the
like tea or coffee and he has—one—t
eight cups balancing on that tray. Wha
Boy, what a mess if he did. That woul
break, wouldn't it?"

One more unexpected sharp curve
the Community School.

While Marlene and I spent the morn
Sherm had been taken to the univer
men with whom he would be associa
the room just ahead of him. Lloyd
bed studying Persian (Farsi) and fee

Sherm burst in, all sunshine, wear
outfit—striped pants, cutaway, and
you really went to a lot of trouble
laughed. Our teen-agers joined in th
looked disappointed.

"I know. The stores are closed every day from one until about four. I'll have to get used to that. May even develop the nap habit myself."

"Mrs. Morgan said the worst days to shop are Friday, Saturday, and Sunday. All Moslem stores close Friday, Jewish shops Saturday, and Sunday all the Christians. You better shop the other days, so there will be more stores open," Marlene advised.

Just then four donkeys, sagging under unwieldy loads, appeared from nowhere in front of us. Their driver lazily wandered along unperturbed as the car all but removed his mount's rear.

"Did you see those bright blue beads around those donkeys' necks? Look quick and you can see." Marlene was urgent.

I turned suddenly and got a glimpse of shimmering blue.

"Say, I know what they are for—to ward off the evil eye. That's what someone told me yesterday. Better get some for myself. I'll need a lot of luck today," said my nervous Marlene.

Goats sallied in and out between cars in the next dingy *kutche* and our driver barely missed one, then another, as we slid from side to side on the seat. Flocks of well-disciplined turkeys marched in front of their herder through the thickest of traffic without so much as a flutter of a single wing.

"Doesn't it just kill you—all these walls so we can't see what's behind them? Makes everything look exact-ly the same. How do people ever find which wall is theirs?" Marlene chattered on, trying her best to divert my mind from the worry of not knowing where we might end our journey. "If a fellow came home drunk he would never be able to find which home is his."

"I notice all the homes are behind walls. Only the shops are out on the streets," I said. "I'm terribly curious to see what's behind them, too. This section around here is the old one of Tehran and they say this is where the important families have lived, and still do. The wealthiest also have homes in Shimran, a suburb of Tehran, in the summer."

"That's where we are going to live, isn't it?"

"I hope so—if we can find a suitable house there."

"Look at that fellow! What is he carrying on his head?" Marlene was hanging out the window. "Looks like tea or coffee and he has—one—two—gosh, about eight cups balancing on that tray. What if he stumbled? Boy, what a mess if he did. That would be a real coffee break, wouldn't it?"

One more unexpected sharp curve and we were at the Community School.

While Marlene and I spent the morning at the school, Sherm had been taken to the university to meet the men with whom he would be associated. We reached the room just ahead of him. Lloyd was sitting up in bed studying Persian (Farsi) and feeling better.

Sherm burst in, all sunshine, wearing a diplomatic outfit—striped pants, cutaway, and the works. "Say, you really went to a lot of trouble for this gag." I laughed. Our teen-agers joined in the hilarity. Sherm looked disappointed.

Close Call for Tea

"What's so funny?" he asked crossly.

"You," we shouted.

"Do you have to wear that every day?" Marlene asked.

"No, just tomorrow. The *Shahinshah* (King of Kings) is conferring an honorary degree on President Conchi of Italy at the university, and we have to appear at the affair.

"Max, you have to wear a hat and gloves, some kind of an afternoon dress." He turned around slowly. "Do you think this outfit looks all right?" he asked dubiously.

"Sure, it's cute," I replied, scrutinizing him. The tails of the coat came almost to the tops of his shoes, and it was big enough for him to have been pregnant without showing. "I guess they think if you are tall you are also fat, but at least the pants are long enough. You look quite distinguished."

At that moment there was a blare of sirens and much commotion from our street-side window. "Fire!" Marlene shouted as we all dashed to the open windows. An array of motorcycle police escorts were racing down the street. A block or two of jeeps, full of soldiers, followed, then assorted types and sizes of cars filled with official-looking gentlemen, and last, one long, sleek, black Rolls-Royce with two men seated in back, followed by another long, slinky black Rolls carrying two women. People were gathered along Pahlavi quietly waving Iranian flags of red, white, and green, and clapping softly. As soon as the entourage passed, we hurried to the lobby to find out what was going on.

Here we were told that it was the Shah, Queen Saroya, President Conchi, of Italy, his wife, and officials of

the Iranian government returning from the official welcoming of the Italian president at the airport. They
were en route to Saderabad (the summer palace) in
Shimran. Our hotel rooms were as good as a seat on
a fifty-yard line, as these parades took place on Pahlavi
Road. This is the beautiful tree-lined four-lane highway which leads from the summer palace to the city.
It was built by Reza Shah (father of the present Shah),
who in 1925 overthrew the weak, long-ruling Kajar
dynasty in an attempt to awaken Persia from her thousands of years of slumber to bring her into the modern
world.

These parades were an almost twice-daily affair for
the next two weeks while President Conchi was a state
visitor. Whenever the Shah leaves his palace the streets
are blocked, nowadays for about twenty minutes, but
previously for an hour or more. He is then safely escorted to Tehran.

The following day Sherm and I dressed to the teeth
and, in company with other visiting American professors from the university, arrived exactly at the appoint-
ed hour for the function. Men in academic robes and
diplomatic outfits were pouring out of their chauffeur-
driven cars. As we confidently went to enter the gates,
guards blocked our path and motioned us away. This
left us nonplused and quite helpless. We couldn't
speak Persian so were unable to explain we were invited guests. Our invitations were shuffled out and
handed to the guards, but they were unimpressed, shook
their heads, spouted a lot of Persian, then ignored us.
Simultaneously, four of us began pantomimes, but the

guards remained unmoved and uncomprehending. At this point one of our American professors arrived who had been in Tehran for three years and spoke enough of the language to present our case.

The verdict was—no reception today! President Conchi had a bad toothache, so it had to be postponed. "Come back tomorrow," was translated to us.

"Seems some announcement could have been made at the university," Sherm grumbled. Wearing that ill-fitting costume out where people could stare at him was getting on his nerves.

"Communications are difficult here, so few telephones, and you will find it isn't considered too necessary to notify people of changes of social plans, as it is assumed they will find out eventually. You will—just as we have," remarked an American professor of two years' experience in Tehran.

A good stiff dose of patience was what I had always needed, and I shall be forever grateful that my sojourn in Iran has taught me this.

The experienced professor said to me, "If you really want to feel at home in Persia, remove the second hand from your watch."

"Tomorrow" we appeared at the university gates, and this time we were promptly and graciously admitted. From then on we were exposed to a most impressive and dignified ceremony.

People quietly took their seats. Approximately thirty minutes after all had been seated, the low conversation ceased. Unobtrusively, the Shah and Queen Saroya walked in amid dead silence, not to the stage, but to the front seats of the auditorium. The audience arose, the national anthem was played, then His Majesty's party and all of us sat down. Italy's president and the leading Persian symphony orchestra of Iran were seated on the stage.

Copies of the text of the speeches had been given to us both in Persian and French. The second language of this country, French, has been included in their school curriculum for years. English is becoming popular among the present generation.

The president of Italy gave a rousing, emotional speech in French, urging the close friendship of the two countries. Since both countries were once the cradle of civilization they should cement their relations, and work together, he orated. With deep and unaccustomed concentration, I pulled out of my foggy mind enough school French to get the gist of the speech.

The Persian orchestra completely captivated me. The music was, indeed, different but haunting. Leading Iranian musicians have told me that their music is complicated. To my untrained ear it seemed discordant, being in minor tones and no melody, as we understand it. Their traditional music is called the science of circles. They have a singular system of writing their music in a circle divided into sections, each section identified with a certain color. Like all their arts, it is intricate.

A beautiful Iranian girl sang. The singing has a tremolo intonation which is almost impossible for foreigners to emulate. Popular entertainers are not socially well accepted as yet in Iran.

The old-style orchestras are composed of kettledrums, oboes, and a trumpetlike instrument. The present classical orchestras feature the *santoor*, which looks to me like a very small portable triangular piano with strings instead of keys. It is played with a special beautifully made plectrum the end of which is usually wrapped in felt. Sounds something like clavichord music with overtones. Sometimes it is played softly, and again wildly with two plectrums.

The reception which followed was dazzling. It was held in the great reception hall of the university. The auditorium, every hall, every place we stepped was paved with the finest and most costly Persian carpets.

Two tables, each one a hundred yards long, were laden with wonderful Persian delicacies, choice fruits, and beautifully arranged flowers. Enormous, fine rock crystal epergnes, the size of hugh inverted chandeliers, ablaze with hundreds of candles, were placed at intervals on the tables.

Small fruit knives and forks, with piles of plates, one on top of the other, made the place settings. This enables several people to stand at the table and eat all they want from a plate, move on, and let others take their turn and a clean plate. The trick is to get yourself to the table in a hurry if you are interested in food. Since it is the custom to stand over the plate and table to eat, you may not get a turn. This method enables a hostess to serve many people without the worry of where to seat them. These stand-up affairs are the most common way of entertaining large groups among the upper-class Iranians.

The Shah and President Gronchi stood together in a tight little corner and everyone moved away, giving them full berth. Not knowing this was to show deference, and was protocol, Sherm and I tagged along with one of the professors (who had become a rather good friend of the Shah's) to the corner where they stood. We thought people should pay more attention to the King. Our Iranian friends looked startled but polite. The Shah speaks excellent English, seems to understand crazy Americans, and is most gracious.

The court band was awaiting him in the courtyard as were his personal guard of the army's tallest men. They are chosen with the greatest of care and must be "the most faithful of the faithful." They are generally recruited from the tribes.

All the formalities of saluting and standing at attention took place outside as the Shah left. Imagine our surprise to hear the familiar strains of the tune Marlene had come to Iran to play, that good old Western music, "In a Persian Market," rendered by the Persian orchestra as the King quietly took his leave.

ALI AZIZI

MY PRIMARY CONCERN WAS TO GET SETTLED IN A HOUSE.
We had been told it usually took from six weeks to
three months to find a suitable one. The thought of
Marlene spending those weeks trying to study in our
cramped quarters and ferreting out strange food from
the hotel dining room, to take for school lunches,
spurred us to try to break the record. Also, there was
the matter of our air freight arriving in a few days
with no place to put it.

The Point Four Housing Office, which was established to guide perplexed American citizens such as
we, gave us a list of available homes, and with an interpreter, Mr. Mostafi, we took off to find our dream
house. There were no listings in Shimran. A great cry
of complaint went up from Marlene and Lloyd. "But
you promised if we would come we could live in Shimran and have a swimming pool. Remember, you absolutely promised," they insisted vehemently.

They were so right. That was when we were safely
on the other side of the world.

We learned very soon that there were lovely homes
in other sections besides Shimran, in downtown Tehran,
and all the suburbs which stretch to the backdrop of
the rugged Elburz Mountains. Finally, everyone agreed

we had to be open-minded and start someplace, so we did.

Upper-class Persian homes, as a rule, are pretentious with tremendous entrance halls, spacious and numerous rooms. Many times the rooms are built without purpose, just one after another. It takes a great stretch of the imagination to figure out which could be used for what. Convenience is never considered because the occupants have servants and don't have to be concerned with saving steps. Another reason is that the close family ties make it imperative to have a house large enough to accommodate all the cousins, aunts, uncles, and sundry relatives who might converge at one time on holidays and family days.

The first home we entered was enormous. After the formalities of a servant opening the gate, we were ushered into a compound about a block square with not one, but two, huge swimming pools set in a Persian garden which seemed so much what I had anticipated that I expected to stumble over Omar Khayyám lolling under a tree with his jug of wine and lady love. The pools were heavily hedged with massive, colorful chrysanthemums and zinnias. Flowering and plain shrubs sprouted over every foot, and a dense army of poplar trees marched too close together all around the compound walls. Gardening is a vital part of Persian life which reveals the high value they put on water and the growing of plants.

To our Western eyes, it seemed like too much of everything squeezed together without plan. This was only because we were ignorant of the meaning of their gardens. The outside world is shut out by high walls and the closely knit household within is protected and sheltered. A garden to the Persian is a place for meditation and for discussion with one's friends. Gardens are made up in magnificent patterns of color with significant meanings connected to the trees, flowers, and colors. For instance, white indicates purity; red, valor; yellow, jealousy; and green, justice. Offensive colors are never placed near the center of the arrangement whether of a garden or a bouquet. Persian gardens are as complex as Persian rugs, to which they have a great similarity.

Another servant let us into the main house. We entered the one room which contained Western furniture. Curtains were drawn, but the very overstuffed, flowered furniture screamed at us. It fought with the garish figures in the heavy draperies and the vivid rugs hung at intervals on the walls, and with the superb Persian carpets piled deep on the floor. Usually, Persians do not care for things as plain as we like them. To them they are much too simple and uninteresting. However, a few are copying our modern trends in furnishings.

"Theese would not be rented vees de furniture. Landlord, he would take dees vees heem," announced Mr. Mostafi. "Veery much money dees teens cost. He not rent dees, only house."

Enthusiastically, we were guided through room after room, none of which had any furniture, only rugs on the floors and stacks of children asleep on them.

"Is this a nursery school?" Lloyd inquired.

Mr. Mostafi looked startled. "No, dees fameely home."

"So many children. Do they all belong here?"

"Yes, yes, veery nize family."

"At least, the children wouldn't go with the house," Sherm consoled me.

I couldn't imagine how we could heat all those rooms with kerosene space heaters. Persians usually heat only one room for the winter. That is practical.

When we got to the kitchen my decision was made, negatively. It was a separate room from the house and just large enough for two people to turn around if they didn't have too much breath in them. There was no counter space, and only an open charcoal and wood-burning type Persian stove, with two huge copper kettles next to it. This, I learned, is a typical Persian kitchen.

Mr. Shiraze, the owner, had now joined us on our tour. He gazed proudly at the kitchen. I looked amazed!

"This house won't do at all. The kitchen is out here and the dining room is on the third floor. The food would be cold by the time it got there and— well—it just wouldn't do."

Mr. Mostafi interpreted to Mr. Shiraze. They both looked bewildered. It was then I learned that this was most desirable to have the kitchen as far away as possible because it kept the pungent cooking odors from the family part of the house. When I objected to the long walk from the kitchen to dining room, they were even more puzzled, and explained that I would have servants to do the walking, so what difference did it make?

My arguments began to sound pretty limp even to me as against their reasoning. It just isn't respectable to have the kitchen as close as we have ours, and for Persians and the way they live, it made perfect sense to me finally. I didn't blame them for thinking I was crazy.

A servant appeared with tea. I was to find this custom prevailed everywhere. In a private home as soon as one is seated, the inevitable servant appears with tea, and, depending on the time of day, fruit or cookies, and always pistachio nuts. In shops and public places tea servers are regular employees. I never visited the university when tea was not being served.

Mr. Shiraze's young wife joined us and, after much gracious hospitality, we said we would think about the house and let them know, and took our leave.

As soon as we got out of the compound Marlene couldn't stand it any longer. "Tell us about all those children. I counted sixteen! That's a lot for one family."

"Dat's good family. Some belong to one wife, some belong to uder wife."

"You mean he has two wives!" Marlene gasped. We all showed great disbelief and pressed Mr. Mostafi to tell us more.

The wife we met was the younger one. An older woman asleep in one room with several children was the first wife. In this case the younger wife ran the home and went out socially with Mr. Shiraze. We

learned later that the three took pleasant walks together in the evenings and often dropped in to call on
American friends of ours.

I looked triumphantly at Sherm. "Aren't you lucky
just to have me? Think of the expense that poor man
has."

"Now that I'm in a Moslem country I could have
three more legal ones," he teased.

"Remember you have to treat them all equally. Mohammed said so. If you have the time to give them
the same attention and luxuries as you give me, I'll
consent," I said magnanimously, feeling quite safe.

Too bad these women hadn't heard of the custom
in southern India where the women can be bigamists.
Might have a mass migration. When they want to get
rid of any unsatisfactory husband, he is notified when
she tosses his shoes out the door. "Any time you get
sold on the Moslem way don't forget there is always
southern India for me," I joked.

Daily we left our hotel after breakfast with Mr.
Mostafi and our rented car to continue our search.
Almost at the same time we were leaving or returning, the Shah and entourage would be en route one
direction or the other. It broke the monotony of house
hunting.

Shimran is where we really wanted to settle and we
finally got a few listings there, but most of our looking was in downtown Tehran. It is a city of two
million, including women and children, who were not
counted until the very recent census. In spite of the
city's size there are many sections where the high walls

shut out the rest of the world, and you can feel far away from the turmoil.

Magnificent homes were mushrooming all over the suburbs. The American advisors sent to advise in fire prevention were transferred to assist in other departments as well, since fires are not common. This is because 95 per cent of the house is brick, with a bit of steel and practically no wood.

Property is very high. Land speculators are doing just as they do in the States, and although the government is making an effort to control them, prices keep soaring. Business-section land prices are comparable with those of similar business sections in the States, and so are the lots in the residential areas. We watched the prices jump by leaps and bounds in the first year in Tehran.

A few homes were being built for speculation with apparent Western appeal so that they could be easily rented to Europeans and Americans. There were few of this type. Persians prefer a two-story house, at least, and convenience is of no importance. We were in and out of many spectacular show places. Marlene's stock exclamation came to be, "What a place for a wedding!"

It was a happy day when we found a house in Shimran, that charming section at the foot of the mountains, about ten miles from Tehran. Foreigners stay here the year round, and that's what we planned to do. Elevation is around four thousand feet so that, although it is desert country, the summers are never too hot, and the winters, although colder than downtown, are pleasant.

The house would suit our family needs and, best of all, was partially furnished. Since we had to buy all of our furniture, which would be a tremendous investment, this appealed.

We started the bargaining. Each day we met in the Housing Office and, through interpreters, proceeded to come to terms. We sat like deaf mutes while the interpreter and landlord spurted fountains of Persian and gesticulated all over one another. Each day the landlord came down a little, but not so much that he would lose face. Higher prices on everything is the penalty for being an American. On houses the Housing Office tries to protect us by not allowing us to pay unreasonable prices. This helps the Iranians keep down their inflation as well.

After four days we were still not at an equitable price. We were discouraged.

The evening of the fourth day a reception was given by the Institute for Administrative Affairs to honor us and two other couples who had just arrived. It was held in the gardens of the American Club. The club had been organized four years before as a spot where Americans could become acquainted with one another. Meals are served, there is a teen-age club, and movies, dances, parties, and sports for all.

As the Iranian professors filed by the receiving line, we were overwhelmed by their courtesy and graciousness. It is a Persian custom, as in Europe, for everyone to shake hands, men and men, women and women, and men and women. The men bow low and radiate warmth and affability. As they went by, Alice Morgan suggested we ask one of them, whom she and Bill considered to be especially diplomatic and reliable, to help us bargain with our stubborn landlord.

Dr. Ali Azizi came up. Mrs. Morgan whispered, "This is the fellow," and gave us a very special introduction.

As soon as we could gracefully break ranks Sherm and I went in search of Dr. Azizi. We found him in deep and animated conversation with friends. He excused himself, stepped aside, and listened to our tale of woe.

"Tomorrow, I will go with you to the landlord," he offered.

"Say, that will be great if you will." Sherm beamed.

We had immediate confidence in him and were relieved to put ourselves in his hands.

As soon as we could get Alice and Bill aside we pummeled them with questions about Dr. Azizi.

"Wonderful fellow," said Bill. "Went to University of Indiana, Columbia, and Queens College. Got his doctorate at the University of Southern California. All this after having graduated from the University of Tehran Law School. He is a judge, too, as well as a professor."

"Doesn't look old enough to be a judge," Sherm said.

"He is in his early thirties, but he has the ability— and comes from the right family. That is most important here—your family—and connections."

"He seems to have a terrific sense of humor," I said.

"Certainly has. You will find the sense of humor in this country almost the same as ours. Ali is very smart. And did you notice he speaks English well?"

Before leaving, we huddled with Dr. Azizi to make final arrangements for the next day. His flashing black eyes perpetually twinkled, and tonight they seemed to mirror everything in the garden. When he became very excited, an illusion of fire seemed to flash from them in all directions. As we came to know him well, it seemed his eyes, no matter how he felt, were always effervescent and usually flaming for a cause.

Ali was to become our dear and trusted friend. Of course we didn't call him Ali until we had known him for months, and long after that he called us by our last names until we gave him permission to use our given ones. It is the Persian way to address friends by their last name. Many Persians who have known one another for years can't bring themselves to address each other by first names.

At three o'clock sharp our room telephone rang. Dr. Azizi was waiting for us in the lobby, the desk clerk said. We had been led to believe the Persians were always late, so we were not ready. He is one of the most punctual persons we have ever known, and this is also true of many other of our Persian friends. We decided people are the same the world over, some are prompt, some are honest, and others are not either one.

"Good afternoon, Mr. Miller and Mrs. Miller." Ali bowed low. "I waited in my car fifteen minutes to make sure I would not be ahead of time. My car is just outside. I have made the necessary arrangements with your prospective landlord, Mr. Naderi, and we will go immediately to his office."

We climbed into his Persian-carpeted Mercedes Benz. This is a very popular car with the upper classes, and most practical for the terrain. After we discussed the weather, I felt someone should make an effort to continue the conversation, so I inquired sweetly, "Do you have any children, Dr. Azizi?"

Sherm and I were sitting in the back seat. He turned around and flashed that captivating smile of his and tactfully replied, "No, I am happy to say that I have not, Mrs. Miller. You see, I am not married."

He had great dignity and could look just as solemn as the judge that he was. His smile faded into his judge's expression. I was slightly disarmed but as usual rushed in when "Oh" would have been enough and said, "Oh, heavens! Then I'm glad you don't have any children."

Ali threw back his head of shiny black hair and laughed amiably. The ice was broken. This opened the floodgates of his joking, prankster nature which kept our spirits high the entire time we lived in Tehran. He was many people, and to all but his closest friends, he kept himself under perfect control, acting the suave, worldly, sensitive gentleman that he was.

Persians do not wear their hearts on their sleeves. I have never known a prouder people. Ali was among the proudest of these.

When we met with the landlord Ali did the talking. We wagged our heads in both directions just in case we should be agreeing or disagreeing. We will

never know what was said, but Ali had bewitched him
into meeting our offer and throwing in a complete
paint job of the entire inside of the house with colors
of our choosing.

"Let us go now to the house and decide on the
colors," Ali suggested.

We were in Tehran and the house was at the far
end of Shimran, but Ali is not one to put off till tomorrow what he can do today. The landlord objected
as he seemed to have pressing business at hand, but
this deterred Ali not one bit. The colors and everything else were settled, and next morning at eleven
we would meet in the Housing Office and sign the contract. All the time we tried to carry on a conversation, runny-nosed, unkempt children swarmed through
the house. Being the curious type, I asked, "And to
whom do these children belong?"

Ali translated, "To the gardener who goes with the
house. He has living quarters down at the end of the
compound. See." He pointed out the window.

"Oh," I said. "Well, we are going to hire our own
gardener, so I hope this one will have no trouble finding
another job."

Mr. Naderi and Ali exchanged words—lots of words
—then Ali said, "He says you have to keep the gardener.
He goes with the house. Will cost two hundred toman
a month. You see, in this country many of us have
retainers, people from our villages or servants born into
the family. It is our duty to take care of them. These
people have only seven children, anyway," he said.

"Seven children!" Sherm gulped. "Since the gardener

is Mr. Naderi's responsibility he will have to figure
out something else for him. We will get our own."

More Persian conversation. "He says this is impossible. There is no other place for the gardener and his
family to live. This is Mr. Naderi's property and he
says the gardener must stay here."

"Just a minute," warned Sherm. "Tell Naderi we
aren't making any such deal. We want the right to
hire any gardener we choose. We have already raised
two children and we aren't about to take on seven
more. The house without the gardener—otherwise the
deal is off!"

Ali and Mr. Naderi went on at great length while
our heads bounced back and forth like tennis balls.
Ali was using all of his persuasive powers.

Eventually, Ali turned to us, "Oh, boy, that was a
hard one." He shook his head. "At first he refused
to give in for any reason, but now he has agreed to
try to find a place for the gardener. He will know
for sure if this can be arranged by your meeting time
tomorrow."

I was so relieved that I could have kissed Ali. Except women never kiss men and vice versa, even their
husbands, in public or before a third party in Moslem
countries.

Things were looking up, that is until about midnight when Sherm became violently ill. It was the
common malady which seems to strike many travelers
at one time or another. The Army hospital does not
send doctors, and he was too ill to be moved. By six
o'clock I got up enough courage to phone the hotel man-

ager, who spoke some English, and beg for help. An Iranian doctor arrived within forty minutes. It seemed there was not much could be done.

I began to worry about signing the lease for the house. I knew how Iranians felt about women's position and to have to deal with one business-wise could easily make the landlord change his mind.

The kind hotel manager came to our room, first to inquire about Sherm, and second to tell us that he had spoken to a rental agent about a house for us, since he wanted to be helpful. The agent was in the lobby.

"My husband is too ill. I couldn't leave now." I said.

Sherm feebly indicated that there was nothing I could do to help him and just in case there was a hitch on the other house I might as well look. When the hotel manager volunteered to have one of the maids stay in our adjoining room, in case Sherm needed anything, Marlene and I decided to go.

The first home we saw was at the very end of Tajrisch (village of the Shah's summer palace). It could have been an estate in the most exclusive suburb of any American city. It was modern to the extreme, the whole house being almost entirely of glass. It was the sort of house you would see in a movie and feel the picture was overdrawn because there were no such houses. There were three enormous pools, all with statues, fountains gushing all over the place, and acres of magnificent gardens. It had fifteen bedrooms. Somehow, I didn't think we would be having that many house guests. The rental price matched the impressiveness. It was fun to have seen.

The next one was also imposing. The grounds seemed literally to cover miles. They extended way beyond the reach of the eye. The landlord spoke English and was quick to tell us that he had two sons who lived in the States and that he went there every year. He was now going for two years and wanted to rent his house. When we stepped onto one of the many balconies I was rather startled to see gorgeous flower displays that seemed vaguely familiar.

The landlord volunteered the explanation. "Dees flowers, all dees is copy of de veery best deesplays at International Flower Show at Los Angeles. For eight year I go see and I come back and I have veery best ones copy. You like?"

"Oh, yes." I became nostalgic. I was back at the good old Flower Show laboring alongside my philanthropic friends of the Assistance League on Première Night. He did not know how close this event was to my heart.

The agent understood very little English, but laboriously I got over to him that all these homes were much too large and expensive for us. It was getting late and we had an appointment at eleven o'clock. Please, would he return us to the hotel.

On the way he turned off Pahlavi. I protested, but he waved it away. Just one more house, he kept insisting, and we would be back in plenty of time. This house he was going to show us was perfect—just what we wanted. I doubted that, but he was driving and we had to go where he went.

He turned merrily into a tiny *kutche* where we

bumped along on coarse gravel, rocks, and holes as
big as half the car. Bricks were strewn in the street
and the *jube* (a running stream by which most of the
country gets its water) ran right down the middle.

He brought the car to a stop and motioned us out.

Most reluctantly I climbed from the seat, giving
the agent my blackest and most scornful look, and with
an air of "you can't make me like it," followed him.
I planned to walk in the door and right out again.
Somehow I shuffled along to the living room, then
found myself on the terrace.

"Oh, Mother. What a dream. It's built just for
us. Look at that sparkling, beautiful pool and the garden. Why, the garden is fabulous! Let's look all through
the house, just for fun."

I did have to admit to myself the garden was breath-
taking. It was formal and perfectly kept. The only
formal garden we had seen. It was not typically Persian
because it had great expanses of grass.

The main part of the house was all on one floor.
The lower level had a large recreation room and an
enormous greenhouse. It was new, very modern, with
all-glass doors opening onto the terrace from every
room except the kitchen and bathroom. The family
bathroom was all white tile, divided into two sections.
Plumbing was Western.

"The bathroom is big enough to hold your bridge
club," Marlene said.

The kitchen also was not Persian. It was very large
and even had some counter space made of the same
tile as the bathrooms.

"I don't want to disappoint you, dear," I remarked to Marlene, "but the price would be too high and Housing would never let us have it."

"Oh, Mother, it would be so wonderful. It doesn't cost anything to dream, does it?"

"After all we have gone through about the other house and having Ali work with the landlord so hard —we just couldn't turn it down now."

I left Marlene off at the hotel and checked on Sherm. He was feeling slightly better. We started telling him about the house we had just seen, but he couldn't stand to hear voices and just nodded that any old house would be all right with him.

When I arrived just five minutes after eleven at the Housing Office, the landlord with whom we were negotiating was not there. No sooner had I sat down than the door opened and in walked our rental agent. He pointed to an older man slumping in a chair across the office from me and through an interpreter I learned he was the owner of the house we had just seen. This startled me. I couldn't then and haven't since figured out how that landlord got there even ahead of me. These Persians are clever people.

I refused to talk with him as I told them I was waiting to sign a contract with another landlord.

"Are you interested in his house? Do you want to discuss it with him?" Mr. Golar, the Housing manager, asked me. "I'll tell you right now, that fellow is the hardest headed landlord in this town. We have dealt with him before and found him impossible. He has held that new house vacant for a year because he can't get his price. It's way out of reason, but just for the hell of it, I'm going to ask him what he is asking for it today."

Mr. Golar summoned an interpreter. Wild gesticulation and loud conversation ensued. It seemed they were raging mad and would soon come to blows. I moved my chair back. This went on and on, and the more furious the conversation, the faster the landlord fingered his beads. I looked with fright toward Mr. Golar, but he sat smiling.

As the story was interpreted to me the first price was ridiculous. He was told I was there to sign a contract with another landlord, thereby playing one against the other. The ornery old fellow began slowly to reduce his price. It has to be slow to keep face. I kept shaking my head "no" and this seemed to help my cause. After half an hour of this the obstinate landlord was evidently now ready to throw in the sponge and rent his house. He had met the price we were going to pay for Mr. Naderi's house.

Here it was almost noon and Mr. Naderi hadn't shown up. I began to have doubts. Perhaps he couldn't make arrangements about the gardener.

"Do you want to work out the contract on this fellow's house?" asked Mr. Golar, motioning to the landlord.

"I don't know what to say. We like this fellow's house ever so much better than Naderi's. The location is wonderful. I'm sure it will be all right with Mr. Miller. Go ahead, let's see what we can work out."

That was the starting bell. The landlord moved in to

the desk with the rental agent behind him. They both dragged out their *tizbahs* and started fingering. At the time I was still unfamiliar with the custom. I thought they were praying and were even enlisting help from Allah against me. It was most disconcerting. They fumbled at the beads, their voices rose and fell, and the interpreter would occasionally bang on the desk.

"Now, is there anything that should be done about the house before you sign?" asked Mr. Golar.

"Well, there were no chandeliers, only light bulbs hanging, but I presume that is only because there are a few finishing touches like that yet to go."

"You have a lot to learn about business dealings here. Unless you put it in the contract, you will have only naked light bulbs."

"Then I insist that he put in beautiful chandeliers in every room in the house."

The landlord stood up and shouted, got red in the face; I was sure he was going to have a stroke.

"He refuses to put in a single chandelier. Says at the price you are getting the house you are stealing it anyway, and chandeliers are very expensive."

That's when I decided this bargaining business was a game for two. Usually I shy away from all such encounters, but I had now made up my mind I wanted that house.

Two hours later I emerged, weak, wiser in the ways of Persian business dealings, and ready to fall flat on my face. I doubted if I had the strength to crawl out the door and find a taxi.

The landlord spun on his heels, refused to shake

hands with me or even look at me, which is a grave insult, and stomped out—but after having signed the contract.

"What's the matter with that old goat?" I asked.

The interpreter laughed. "You're a woman and they are not used to doing business with women; and in the second place, you got the chandeliers and other odds and ends which he had no intention of giving you. He has lost face."

Marlene was overcome with joy when I announced that we had her dream house signed and sealed. This pepped Sherm up enough so that he grunted an affirmation and was able to keep down a sip of water after that. Lloyd was there waiting his turn.

He said proudly, "Well, I've gotta job. Manager of the Commissary Warehouse. Got sixteen coolies under me. They can't speak English, but I'll know enough Farsi in five days—that's when I start—to get along. And I manage the Embassy refreshment stand at nights. That's a separate job."

"Why, that's great," I said. Lloyd had been searching everywhere for a job because he would be unable to attend the University of Tehran (since it was all in Persian) and jobs for young foreigners were few.

"With your gift for languages, you will get by," I told him. And he did learn to speak Persian fluently, to read and write it in a matter of a few months. This is an accomplishment. He thought their shorthand type of writing, starting from right to left, was a cinch. I thought it was impossible!

"Now, listen to what I have to say." Marlene was

impatient. "They called from Community School—
and"—she waited for effect and reaction—"and—I'm
in!"

"What a relief! Now our only worry is to get your
father on his feet and then to explain to Ali about
the house without hurting his feelings." I didn't have
to worry long about it because Ali telephoned. I had
hoped Sherm would feel well enough to do the talking,
but he didn't.

Ali began, "Did you get the house?"

I hesitated, "You know, Mr. Naderi never did come."

"He wasn't supposed to come unless the Housing
Office called him. You didn't understand? He was to
be there at eleven o'clock if they called."

Then I told him what I had done.

"Sounds great! I didn't like the other house. Why
you want it anyway?" Such a diplomat—Ali.

YOU DON'T KNOW PERSIANS

ALI TELEPHONED TO INQUIRE ABOUT SHERM'S HEALTH for the next two days. On the third day he appeared in person.

He stepped briskly into the room and bowed as he inquired as to our health. Iranians are a medium-sized race and by their standards he would be considered of medium stature. He had been a sprinter in high school. His figure was athletic with muscles hard as flint. Persians are excellent at sports such as horseback riding, wrestling, weight lifting, ping-pong, tennis, volleyball; and soccer is becoming popular.

His sparkling eyes and winning smile flooded the cheerless room as he presented us with four lovely Persian vases for our new home.

"How thoughtful of you. They are charming, and we can truthfully say the only things we have to make a house a home." The rest of the family was also touched by this warm gesture. It was wonderful to have such an attentive friend in this different land. He was an invaluable interpreter because, as yet, we knew just a few basic Persian words. Most of the working class speak only their native tongue. How we wished we had known we were coming soon enough to have studied the language.

"If Mr. Miller feels like it tomorrow, I come and take you for a ride. How about it?"

"I'll feel like it," Sherm's voice quavered. "I'm fed up with this room. I want to get out of here, get settled, start to work."

"O.K. I come in the morning and show you Tehran."

True to his word Ali arrived at ten in the morning, right on the button.

Happily, Sherm and I left the dreary room and climbed into the back seat of Ali's car. Not, however, until we had met his cousin, a major in the Iranian army, who was sitting in the front seat. He was young, handsome, and important-looking in his uniform.

Instantly, we took off. Literally, because when you ride with Ali you take off like a jet and ride the entire journey at a comparable speed.

After we came to know him well, I asked him the reason. His explanation was a bit unusual. "You see I am a direct descendant of the prophet Mohammed —on both sides of my family. My mother and father are second cousins. Mohammed looks out for me all the time. Any time you want a special favor call on me and I'll call on Mohammed." He laughed gaily.

"Are you kidding?"

"No, I'm serious. I honestly am his direct descendant. My grandfather was a great and respected religious leader who interpreted and translated the Koran from Arabic to Persian. Both he and my father were respected leaders and wore the black turban which signifies their direct descendancy from Mohammed. These kind of people are highly honored here."

"And who protects the Christians who ride with you?" I humbly asked.

"Don't worry. I'll call on Mohammed to include you infidels whenever you are with me."

At first I kept my eyes shut and sat stiff as a poker, and then I couldn't bear to miss the fascinating street scenes, so I forced myself to look. Women in black *chador* ambled indifferently across the street. Children and ragged workmen waited until we were almost upon them, then they would defiantly step in front of the car. Time after time I expected the donkeys, flocks of turkeys, stray goats, and people to be flying in all directions, but by some miracle, evidently Mohammed's watchfulness, in the two years we rode with Ali this never happened.

When I mustered enough courage to drive myself, after sixteen months, then is when I really appreciated Ali's great driving ability, his accurate eye and good judgment. It must have taken much undivided concentration to appear to drive so carelessly but still, in the final analysis, be so safe.

We headed toward South Tehran and, after seeing some famous landmarks, arrived at the major's home. His precious little daughter with wide, dark eyes greeted us at the door with a bouquet of flowers. A servant appeared and escorted us to the living room. The major summoned his wife. She was very young, and a striking beauty. Sherm's pale, drawn face took on some color as soon as he saw her.

Since they had not talked with any Americans before and did not speak English, Ali was kept busy interpreting. Both the major and his wife are cousins to Ali, and they in turn are cousins to one another. Marrying cousins is common practice. The intention is to link families together, combining the wealth, influence, and power, and increasing the security of each. Family ties are so great that to keep all of this together by making uncles and aunts, also in-laws, is an enviable accomplishment.

Refreshments were brought in. The inevitable tea, cakes, pistachios, and a popular pudding made of rice and saffron. Conversation through Ali was most cordial and pleasant.

Ali got up and began wandering around the house. He sauntered into the dining room, where a glistening refrigerator stood in all its glory. He inspected it, then asked us to join him in the inspection. This seemed odd and at first we hesitated, but he insisted. After poking our heads all through it, Ali smiled *that* smile and asked, "Would you like to borrow this while you are here?"

"Why, that's very nice, but we can't take these people's refrigerator away from them," Sherm said with surprise.

"Go ahead, take it. It's O.K. Major is being transferred to Isfahan. You use it while he is gone. He won't need it, anyway."

"Well, now, it would be a marvelous break for us. How much does he want for the rental?"

Ali looked perplexed, then interpreted to the major, who looked even more baffled. Nobody answered us. Ali began roving around again. He pointed to the dining-room table. "Would you like that, too?" He wagged his finger at the kitchen table, then a wardrobe. Finally the entire living-room furniture had been included, overstuffed chairs, sofas, coffee and end tables.

"Take it all," he gestured. "He won't need it for a year. In our country when you aren't using something, you let your friend use it." Then he looked at the fine rugs. "Take them, too."

Sherm and I were covered with confusion and completely confounded. We looked helplessly at one another. We had been told how very generous the Persians are. When you admire something very much, which belongs to them, it is traditional to offer it to you. More often than not the giving of expensive items, however, is just an offer, nothing more. One of Sherm's Iranian students in the States had told us a story which was now floating through my mind. One of his friends had offered an Englishman one of the most precious rugs in Iran, as the Englishman had admired it so enthusiastically. The friend insisted that the offer be accepted. The Englishman finally sent his servants to pick up the rug. He got the rug but lost a friend. I didn't want this to happen to us.

Since women don't have much status in Iran, I decided this was just the time for me to take advantage of my newly acquired Iranian position. I smiled challengingly at Sherm. He grimaced at me for an expression. I looked blank and remained silent—for once.

He began humming and hawing. "Now, that is certainly generous of your cousin. Are you sure he knows you have just offered us all his furnishings?"

"Sure, he understands. Fine with him. He wants you to have it. All of it. Just take it."

"He must be going to rent his house. He could get more if he rented it furnished."

Ali shrugged. "Guess so. But you have a house and you need furniture. He doesn't need it. You take it."

"Well, of course, we wouldn't consider accepting it for nothing. See if you can work out a deal with him whereby we can rent it for the year. Everything except the rugs, that is. We don't want to be responsible for them."

Much Persian flowed. The major and his wife were bewildered.

Ali turned to us. "You know what they say? They say it is just what they always hear about Americans, always thinking of money, always materialistic. You don't know Persians! They are your friends. They cannot accept your money. This is not a business offer."

"Since they have never seen us before, how can they consider us friends?" Sherm was quizzical.

"You are my friend, they are my family, so you are their friend also."

My interpretation would have been if we had taken something for nothing then we would definitely be materialistic. Oh, well, just another difference in cultures.

Sherm said, "I guess we don't know Persians but that's what we're here for—to get to know them. Now we want to do the right thing by these people." Sherm addressed his remarks to Ali. "You have lived in the States a long time so you know Americans. Now, how

will this go over? Tell them if they will accept our
check, we will gladly take their furniture and they
will be doing us a great favor."

Sherm sat right down and wrote out a check for
what he thought would be fair in the States, so would
be doubly so here. Ali looked at the check, smiled all
over, and handed it to the major with an explanation
which was evidently of the amount. The wife began
to cry softly and the major to perspire profusely. Soon
he dashed out of the room and returned with an exquisite and costly camel bone box (one of their prized
possessions) and presented it to me.

This threw me for a loss. I couldn't figure out for
the life of me what I should do now.

"Dr. Azizi," I pled, "why is he giving me this precious
gift? I don't think I should accept."

"He feels you are doing him a big favor by allowing him to store his furniture with you. To them it
is a lot of money you gave them. They don't understand you. Such crazy Americans, they think."

"I guess this works both ways. We don't know Persians, they don't know Americans. Explain to them
how much we appreciate their making this furniture
available to us. The money is just a favor in return,"
Sherm said.

"I'll explain. You get the furniture, he gets the
money." Ali began to show strain. "Very hard to explain Americans, but I do my best." And he tried.

After a long conversation (for some reason it seems
to take ten times as long to say things in Persian) it

was arranged that we would have the movers there the next day.

Bright and early next morning the major and furniture arrived at our home. He had accompanied the movers to insure good protection. First thing they began to haul in carelessly were stacks of beautiful dishes. We had accepted the china cabinet but had no idea these were inside. Now, we would have enough dishes for entertaining. When I saw the valuable silver pieces I persuaded the major to take them back (through pantomimic argument).

When the movers set to work, then I understood why the major had come along. They managed to take off corners of all the doors, bang into every two walls out of four as plaster crumbled all over the floor. I was dubious about the furniture holding together until they got it placed. When Sherm could stand it no longer he threw off his coat and pitched in to help. The workmen were aghast! In a stage whisper I said, "You are losing face—in fact, you have no face left at all. Remember, customs are different here."

He continued to sweat and strain and was left to do most of the moving solo, as the paid helpers looked on with interest. They conversed among themselves, and how I wish we could have understood their remarks. The major seemed too shocked to protest.

The master was good and tired as he flopped into a chair after everything had been placed, exactly two and a half weeks to the day since we arrived in Tehran.

The sequel to this episode is that after eight happy, comfortable months with the major's furniture, he was transferred back to Tehran. This threw us into a panic. At that time we thought we were staying just for one year, which would give us less than four months to be without furniture. We could either invest a small fortune and furnish our big house for this short time or become completely Persianized and live without any at all—just have rugs—but then, where would we get rugs?

As usual Ali came to the rescue and offered to buy a house full of furniture for us and allow us to rent it from him. We protested that this was beyond anything expected of any friendship but he kept assuring us, "Don't worry, don't worry about a thing. You will have furniture. Leave everything to Mohammed and me."

Bless his great big wonderful heart. We did, and it was the major's again. He convinced the major and his wife it would be a very profitable business deal if they would rent to us for another year, and that among their relatives they could get together enough furniture to see them through. He led off by giving them his own refrigerator and by buying a new one for his home. The major came to assure me that it was a happy arrangement by bringing me a gift.

Ali had the natural faculty of being able to smooth troubled waters. One of the subjects he taught at the university was Human Relations, and I am sure it was never taught anywhere in the world with more mastery.

Three months later the major was suddenly transferred again to Tabriz for an undetermined length of time—possibly years. He sent word that we had done him a tremendous favor as otherwise he would have been stuck trying to figure out what to do with his furniture.

From then on we left everything we couldn't solve in the hands of Ali and Mohammed.

Now we could start housekeeping in earnest. Draperies would have to be made. One wall of every room, except kitchen and baths, had glass doors, so this would be a project. We would be living in a goldfish bowl for some time. Marlene quickly solved this problem for her room and shared her improvisation with us.

"Everybody hang all your clothes along the tops of the windows. Keeps people from staring in. Come see." She motioned and we followed. She had made a chain of hangers up and down and across so that every inch was covered by a most interesting array of a four-season wardrobe, from sun suits to formals.

"Not bad," we agreed, and did the same in our bedroom.

Since the floors are of tile many people leave them uncovered. We decided it was better to have something on the floors to kill the sound of clicking heels and for warmth in winter. Zelu was our selection for this. I would say it is a very good quality of burlap, comes in lovely colors, and gives a most modern effect. Only Americans and fifth-class citizens of Iran would be caught dead using it.

First investment an Iranian ever makes is in a rug. The tribesmen, peasants, everyone owns rugs. When they move they take all their belongings, the most important being their rugs, sling them on their backs, and are off. Even servants can't imagine life without carpets. A man's castle is his rug. Wherever he throws his rug is home.

Ali kept insisting that we accept the major's carpets. He must have had to do a lot of apologizing when he brought Iranian friends to visit us. Here we were, Americans, and of course all Americans are very rich, but still we had no rugs. In fact, so many of our Persian friends offered to lend us costly carpets, for which we didn't want the responsibility, that we rented some. Unfortunately, we had grown used to the modern look of plain-colored zelu and our lowly status, so we returned them after a while.

We went all out and had a lot of fun using colors we never would have the courage to try for a permanent abode. We did the family room with red corduroy draperies, red zelu, red plastic, modern chairs against cream-colored walls. Sounds cheerful, doesn't it? It was, and was especially effective when the compound was covered with snow in the winter. The rest of the house, living room, dining room and all, we did in our usual conservative color schemes.

Our next problem was finding a servant. While still at the hotel we had interviewed innumerable ones and were delighted when we were lucky enough to get Tooba. She had come highly recommended by the driver of an American friend. She spoke some English, which made her a special treasure. Also she had been trained by Americans, so knew our eccentric ways. Her dress was modern, no *chador*, just a scarf thrown over her head when she went out. Americans and other foreigners call their women help *badjis*. *Badji* means "sister" in Turkish, and nobody knows how we corrupted it into a name for a servant, but they seem to like it and it does convey warmth. Now we had our *badji*.

IT COULDN'T HAPPEN

OUR SETTLING PROCESS WAS GOING SLOWLY BUT STEADI-
ly when we celebrated the third morning in our house
by Marlene awakening us abruptly — and on Sunday
morning, too.

She had quietly sneaked into our room, but not without awakening me. I can detect the breathing of a
body almost three blocks away, although sound asleep.
In an unquiet voice she whispered to me, "Are you
awake?"

Sherm flounced over and slightly raised his head.
"Well, we are now," and he rolled back and fell asleep
again.

"Mother, someone was in my room last night and
took my necklace, the one I wore to the party and
left lying on my dresser. They took it out of the box.
The box was on the floor next to the door—empty."

"Sit down on my bed," I told her as I put my arm
around her. "Now, dear, I know we have been told
all sorts of weird tales about the sneak thieves and how
clever they are. I can't say that I believe all of them.
It's just entertaining conversation. As I have said, I
feel safer here than in the States where burglars often
kill. Usually, in this country, they are unarmed. You
are such a light sleeper that no one could have opened

your door without your hearing him. The way these doors squeak—it's impossible. Another thing, we have little old Tippy out there guarding us." Everybody has a dog or dogs in Tehran for protection. We had been presented with one the day we moved in. He was a small, white mongrel, but could outbark any dog I've ever heard. In fact, he rarely stopped barking.

"I don't care. Someone was in my room."

"Tippy didn't make one sound. The house is locked tight as a drum. Go back and get some sleep, then when we are all more wide awake, we will look for your necklace." I sank back onto the pillow and prepared to sleep.

"Can't you wait until morning for all that yakking?" Sherm complained.

"It really is morning, about seven o'clock," I countered.

"All right, if nobody wants to listen to me, but just come and look for yourself and see the box lying right by the door, and the necklace gone. What a family! Nobody cares if we've been robbed—nobody but me." She flipped out the door in a huff.

Sherm stretched and groaned. "We just can't take her around where people are telling tales about robberies. It has preyed on her mind. Ridiculous things like wallets being taken right from under a pillow and sheets slipped right off the bed when a fellow is asleep—just figments of someone's imagination. Of course, we did see the Bennet house right after all their rugs were taken and furniture cleaned out with eight people and two dogs sleeping in the house. Then that woman up the street who had all her jewelry stolen by the servant, but the police caught her and found it hidden in that loaf of bread. Anyway, I would like to see someone come into this room and take anything. With you around we don't even need a watchdog. It seems to me every time I breathe you sit up in bed and holler! 'What's the matter?' Do you ever really sleep?"

After a pause, he continued, "Well, guess if we are going to church we will have to get up." Sherm yawned and dragged out of bed.

Lazily he put on his clothes, pulling on the pants he had worn the night before. They were hung on a hanger just above his head from an improvised wardrobe. Deliberately he unfolded the money belt which he had just taken from his pocket. Suddenly the strangest expression crept over his face, then he turned white.

"Marlene!" he called to the next room.

"What?" came a reluctant and exasperated answer. "What do you want?"

"Come here," Sherm demanded in an excited voice.

"What for?"

"Come here—and don't ask any questions."

"What's the matter with you?" I demanded.

"My money—it's gone—all of it out of my money belt. The rent money—I cashed a check to pay six months in advance—it's gone!"

"You're kidding. You just can't be serious." My heart sank.

Marlene forced herself to come in at this point.

"Did you say you lost a necklace last night?" Sherm rushed on.

"That's what I said, but you said I didn't. Why?"

"I'm sorry, dear, but you must be right. My money belt has been taken from my pocket, relieved of the money, folded neatly, and returned. How anyone could open these new squeaky doors and work directly over my head without my hearing is a mystery. And with your mother in here, too—it just isn't possible."

"Oh, no!" I quickly remembered that Lloyd had given Sherm all the take from the Embassy refreshment stand the night before for safekeeping. "The money—from the Embassy—— Good heavens! Was that in your belt, too?" I choked.

Sherm started crawling under his bed. I thought he had snapped. He pulled out a shoe, and with a big sigh of relief murmured, "It's here, the Embassy money. I put it in my shoe under the bed. They didn't get that."

Then I remembered something else. "The other half of that check you cashed you gave to me. It was in my purse right here by the side of my bed. I delved shakily into the purse's contents, pulled out my money and with relief saw that it hadn't been touched.

I swung around and sucked in another deep breath. My stone marten stole was still hanging on a rod next to my bed.

We related our tale of woe to Tooba. She stood motionless, showed no feeling, and said she knew nothing about it. All she knew was that when she came to the kitchen the electrical current had been cut, so there was no electricity.

"Oh, they cut the wires so we couldn't turn on the lights if we heard noises," Sherm declared.

"Poor little Tippy, I wonder if he is all right." With that Marlene galloped to the front gate. She returned carrying a peacefully sleeping little dog.

This was so abnormal for Tippy, I felt sure he had been tossed a piece of opium-spiked meat. I had been told this was often the way dogs are taken care of before a robbery.

We called Mohammed, the gardener. He could shed no light on the robbers.

Marlene banged the metal waste basket on her floor, which was just above Lloyd's sleeping head in the room below. This was to be the morning signal for awakening him from that time on. After a long delay he came, rubbing his eyes drowsily, still in somewhat of a stupor.

"Why did you have to wake me? I'm tired, working on two jobs, and this is the only morning I have to sleep."

Marlene blurted out the story in fits and starts. This brought him out of his daze. Lloyd always imagined himself to be a detective; this was his challenge.

He went from door to door and window to window, making a search of a possible means of entry, with the rest of us following. After some time Tooba reluctantly volunteered, as we were about to climb to the roof, that she saw Marlene's big travel purse up there.

"When?" I quickly asked.

After some hesitation she said, "When me go see lights no go."

Marlene dashed to the roof and returned carrying an empty travel purse and with tears streaming down her face. "My souvenirs—all my beautiful bracelets and jewelry that I collected all over the Orient—are gone —everything is gone!"

"That's absolutely terrible," I cried. "Where was your purse?"

"At the side of my bed," she blubbered. "I always kept it there so no one would take it."

Mohammed stood witnessing this emotional episode, then indicated that he would call the landlord and the police. He did, and in a while a solitary police-man arrived, trudged through the house, disinterestedly looked us over, and left.

When we asked the servants if he was going to do something about it, they shrugged their shoulders.

Lloyd had continued his detective work on his own. He clattered down the stairs from the roof into the hall where we all stood. "Come look. It's an inside job. The window in the top of the door going onto the roof is broken and glass all over the place. How-ever, the putty has been carefully removed from the inside—get this—the inside—and the glass has fallen so that it couldn't have been done from the outside." He glared at the uncomprehending servants.

We scrambled up the stairs and, sure enough, he was right. None of the rest of us would probably have noticed these fine points.

"I'm going down to the Hansens and call Ali. I

know he will be able to do something about it," said
Sherm, and he stomped out. The Hansens were the
other Americans on our *kutche* and they had the great
luxury of a telephone.

It seemed Sherm had barely walked into the house
again when we heard Ali's unique automobile horn
going full blast. He jumped out and announced that
he had talked with the Chief of Police and he would
be right up himself.

The Chief of Police arrived with six other policemen
and took over. They went over the place with more
finesse and detail than Sherlock Holmes would have
ever thought possible. The only thing they didn't do,
which we felt would have been helpful, was to take
fingerprints. The minutes grew into hours and I thought
perhaps they planned to stay with us forever. Then
I began to worry about the possibility of the police
being accomplices, which I had heard was often true
in this country, and I knew this to be a fact, too,
occasionally, in our own country. For sure they had
the house well cased for any future reference.

We were all questioned through Ali, then Mohammed and Tooba were carted off to the police station.
Mohammed was released by nightfall, but Tooba was
required to go every day for four days. Evidently
she was given the third degree from morning until night
because she would arrive home in hysterics and claim
that she had not eaten all day and that they were perse-
cuting her. She sobbed and cried and tore at my heart-
strings.

At my insistence, Sherm begged Ali to contact the

police chief and ask him to leave Tooba alone. I knew she was innocent and I couldn't bear to have her go through this ordeal.

They claimed they had to carry out their duty so, unmoved, they had her come still the next day. This time she came back and put on a most convincing act, claiming she was losing her reputation because some friends had seen her at the police station and her career would be finished. Besides, she could see we did not trust her, and she could never work for us under such a cloud. With this I paid her a month's salary and told her to go home and recover. She indicated that if she left our employ the police would, no doubt, leave her alone, and also she said she would be afraid to stay in our home since we had had this robbery.

To see her in such a state had unnerved me much more than the robbery itself.

Tooba left and we never saw her again, but we heard about her.

A few days later, an American woman, a stranger to me, came to my door and introduced herself as Mrs. Layton. She asked if I had a *badji* by the name of Tooba. I invited her in and she unraveled the story about our mutual *badji*. At the time she was working for us, she actually was in the steady employ of Mrs. Layton. She had announced to her that she had a sick aunt whom she had to attend and would be gone for a few days. She returned to Laytons after I had allowed her to leave, and had stolen all the Laytons' jewelry and money she could find over a period of three days, then disappeared.

Mrs. Layton and I reported this to our Embassy in the hope that other Americans would not be taken. We deducted, Mrs. Layton and I, without any outside help, that Tooba and the driver, who had recommended her, were in some sort of a professional ring together. The driver would find her a job with an unsuspecting American, and together they would make the robbery, probably dividing the loot.

Although neither of us ever saw the stolen articles again, we knew we had found the culprit. Luckily for her, we never saw Tooba again either, but we gave her a good tongue-lashing, and sentenced her *in absentia* —the two of us. Tooba—too bad.

HOGI BADJI

OUR FRIENDS WERE VERY HELPFUL IN FINDING US
another *badji*. It is important to have servants in Iran
because it is necessary to have someone in your home
all the time. Even if you choose to do your own work,
you need a house sitter.

Hogi came to us through a *badji* of a friend of a
friend.

As I opened the gate in response to the bell, I wasn't
expecting what I saw. When I swung the gate and
her apparition appeared, my first impulse was to slam
the gate and flee. She was the homeliest mortal I have
ever seen. Vampira is a ravishing beauty by comparison. Her hair hung in great, long, black chunks all
around her face, complete with snarls. Before I had
a chance to retreat, she grabbed me and smothered
me with kisses. This was, indeed, a surprise, as that
emotion is certainly not wasted on strangers in Iran.

She squeaked, "I will teach you to speak Farsi."
That's what I thought she said from my limited understanding of Persian. She motioned to the *kutche* and
by sticking out my horrified face, I saw a small truck
loaded with her belongings. I had only expected to
have an interview.

We were desperate for a servant so I could leave

the house and find some more furnishings. When I saw the luggage, I knew we had one.

She had brought a friend along, "to help her move in," she said. They carried load after load to the room previously used for servants. The room was small, her belongings many, so there was, finally, barely enough room for Hogi to squeeze in.

Hearing Sherm's driver screech the brakes of the car, I knew the master had arrived.

"Hogi," I said, "Agha Miller" and motioned her to open the gate. I thought this would be an unexpected jolt for Sherm after a frustrating day's work. It was!

Hiding behind the grillwork, I could see his expression. He stood transfixed for a moment as if frightened into a trance. Suddenly I began to fear the shock was too much for him. I speedily appeared and smiled my sweetest smile.

"What's this, a gag?" he asked suspiciously. At that moment Hogi snatched his hand and kissed it at least ten times.

"No, it's our new *badji*," I warbled.

"You're kidding, I hope. I thought you made her up on purpose for a joke." He was incredulous.

"This is the one who was coming for an interview, but she moved in, bag and baggage, so all we can do is give her a try."

Hogi beamed like a proud mother hen, fortunately not understanding a word of our English.

All we knew about Hogi was that she came from a very backward village, had been one of four wives, and had recently been discarded. I could understand why her former husband could go on living without her.

Dinner was in the process of being prepared before she arrived, but she insisted on taking over the minute she strode into the kitchen. As I showed her where things were she began busily to taste the contents of the simmering pans by slurping up the food and returning the spoon to the pot. I explained, by pantomime—words failed me even in English—that in this house we did not taste the food and then put the spoon back into it. I found out how well this message got over when she began dishing up the dinner. She repeated the performance and ate off each of our plates before serving us. From now on, I would do all the cooking and serving, I announced.

Hogi had reputedly worked for Americans. Not much American had rubbed off on her.

She was superstitious, like many of the lower classes, especially villagers. She did our washing by hand in the bathtub. She pounded the clothes with a stick until they were not only clean but full of holes. A washing machine even in the wealthiest homes is a rarity. Most people in Iran wash their clothes by pounding. In the villages there is often no soap, and sand is used in lieu of it. In Tehran the poor classes wash dishes and clothes in the running streams (*jubes*).

This was the sort of life Hogi had grown up in, washing and cooking with *jube* water. By the *jubes* the average people live. This is their water supply which runs from the mountains along the side of the roads. One woman will be washing a baby's bottom, one next to her will be washing her dishes, then a few feet away the family laundry will be scrubbed.

The main section of Tehran now has city water piped into the homes for those who can afford it. In the suburbs we have our own wells, but the majority of people have no more water in their homes than they can carry in one day by hand.

The friend who came to help Hogi move in arrived day after day for five days. When she left in the evenings, Hogi instructed me to pay her—and well— for her help. Finally I realized I was being taken and balked on the fifth night. Weeping and wailing ensued, and much Persian was flung at me. However, this well-executed scene left me unmoved. I figured no money, no friend, and we would be rid of her. No such luck. She appeared the next morning, greeted me affectionately, and joined Hogi at her meals, at their innumerable cups of tea, and always they shared the same hubble-bubble pipe (*hookah*).

In Hogi's defense I must say she did iron well, although Sherm was slightly nonplused to find his Cooper jockey shorts, beautifully and stiffly starched, standing by themselves on his bed.

The friend always left with her arms loaded with flowers from our garden. Not until I missed my very fine scissors did I make an issue of it.

"Have you seen my scissors?" I asked Hogi in my own version of Esperanto, which was a mixture of English, Farsi, French, Italian, and pantomime. She dragged them out from under a pan and handed them to me. They showed signs of flower clipping. The

blades were dull, nicked, and useless. I shook my head
and in a five-minute drama enacted my displeasure.
Just as I was reaching the climax, Mohammed appeared,
bowing and pleading.

"Madame," he said, pointing to Hogi. Through his
excited chatter and motioning I knew he was showing
his displeasure with her friend for raiding his prized
rose garden. He insisted that I come to see the damage, which I did. It was pathetic to discover his well-
tended bushes hacked in every direction. I commiserated
with him and promised I would see to it that it did
not happen again.

Ali's welcome horn blasted at the end of this scene.
He stepped inside to a noisy ruckus from Mohammed's
quarters. Hogi stamped in shouting and I implored,
"Please, Ali, interpret. Find out what's going on." He
did.

"It's like this," he said to us, "Mohammed's sister
came to call with her new baby. Hogi was making
disparaging remarks about it—called it a black baby.
Among the peasants when a mother has a girl baby
she will often say she has given birth to a black baby.
She means her own face is black with shame because
she has given birth to a girl instead of a boy. You see,
it is believed that women are weak and that through
them dishonor may come upon a family. There is the
responsibility of getting them married off, too. Often
congratulations on having a girl are 'May Allah be kinder
to you next time.' We have another saying, 'As quiet
as a house in which a daughter has just been born.'
It's a proud mother who has boys. My mother has

always been able to hold her head high because she had five boys."

Hogi went on yelling through Ali's translation to us until she got his attention.

"Hogi gave advice on what the woman was to do next time, so she would be sure to have a boy. It was a different superstition than the sister knew so they had an argument," Ali said.

"What was Hogi's advice?" I asked.

"She told the woman that she should have eaten three dates on the third day so the next baby may be a boy. Also that she must go to the bath later on the same day, when a woman who has given birth to a boy baby is present, and have her throw milk on her so that her next born will be a son. Mohammed's sister claimed she saw a needle before the baby was born— instead of a pin—so she couldn't help its being a girl." He slapped his forehead. "Oh, they are having all kinds of arguments about their different superstitions."

"Do you believe all those superstitions, Ali?" I innocently asked.

An injured look came into his face. "After all, Mrs. Miller, I hope I am educated and enlightened beyond that. No question about it, though, boys are preferred here. For myself I rather have girls. I think little boys are brats. My nieces are sweeter than my nephews. I just told Hogi to mind her own business and let everybody have girls because I think they are better anyway. Now she won't speak to me. She is raving because she thinks I am a madman." Ali doubled over with laughter.

Mohammed's wife appeared to defend her sister-in-law and flooded the room with words. Ali told us: "This is the big day. They are taking the baby to the bath and Hogi was spoiling everything with her suggestions. If it is a girl she gets her first big bath on the eighth day, if a boy on the tenth. It's a big occasion for celebrating. The mother, friends, and midwife all go to the bath."

"Tell us what happens when they get to the bath."

"Since I've never been a mother, I don't know, but I'll ask Mohammed's wife." He did.

"She says," he continued, "that they lather the baby with soap, then dip it head first three times into hot water. Since it's the first big bath, they think they have to cleanse it from all its impurities. After it is washed, she says they put charcoal on its eyelids to make it beautiful."

"Mohammed's baby boy—what you call him, Reza? —has an earache, and Hogi insisted that they put hot ashes into the diaper to cure it. They had another superstition maybe just as ineffective, but there is a difference of opinion. They did agree upon a small piece of jade which they moistened and stuck into Reza's abdomen to stop his colic."

In his suave way, Ali placated all concerned and sent them all about their business.

Life with Hogi was an experience! She wore a small pouch tied so tightly around her upper arm that the arm was always swollen from lack of circulation. The pouch was tied with many colored ribbons and filled with all kinds of slips of paper. Each morning she dipped one of these papers into lemon juice and swallowed it. On my inquiry as to why, the answer was always "for good luck." One day she went through a special routine and ate two whole pages of Persian writing. She explained this had something to do with her divorce and she was following the instructions of a dervish.

I had almost reached the end of my rope with her when I walked in and saw her scrubbing the bathtub with my toothbrush and realized that this was a daily ritual, that I, too, had been using the same brush. I forcefully tried to get over to her the great error she had made, but she shook her head and acted as if she thought I was insane. Evidently she felt each article should be used for many things. She cut the tops off the precious asparagus, threw it away, and cooked the stocks. She was never convinced that the tops were better and refused to cook them.

We asked Ali to join us for tea and I waved Hogi to her room as I wanted some peace and quiet.

As we sat on the terrace and talked, the sweet, sticky smell of Hogi's water pipe wafted up from her room. We had become used to it, but we still thought it was strange-smelling tobacco.

"What kind of tobacco does that old gal use in that water pipe, anyway?" Sherm asked of Ali.

Ali flashed that ingratiating smile of his and, with a twinkle in his eye, said, "That's not tobacco. That's opium. Sometimes they mix it with the tobacco."

"Opium!" I cried. "How could she do such a thing? It's illegal."

"That's right, but there are still ways to get it at a price. Neighboring countries raise it—Afghanistan, Turkey—for medicinal purposes, as we did up until two years ago, but just as happened here, it's hard to control. We have it being smuggled from those borders now besides coming from the poppy fields behind our mountains. We grew opium in our villages, as most everyone did. It was legal and made us rich. However, our government realized it was out of hand, so all the fields were destroyed. We are hard on the peddlers now and have places to help cure those who are curable."

"Well, I am not going to have an addict in our house. I knew she was strange and maybe this is part of the reason. Always felt uneasy around her."

"Maxine thought she was going to be able to do something about her hair until she found out it was a wig. She never seems to get it quite on, and never straight." Sherm chuckled.

That day we parted company with Hogi and her room full of possessions forever.

Next came Eshra. She was four feet tall, neat and clean and efficient. Had worked several years for Americans. She didn't cook—only a few Persian dishes, *pillo* and kebab. Her great fault was that she was undependable. She regaled me about her former husband, who left her flat, with three children to raise. Never would she marry again. She told me endless stories about how dreadful were Persian men. Almost half of each week she didn't come to work. When she did appear, it was always the excuse of illness for herself or one or all of her children. My Iranian friends advised me not to pay her on the days she was absent. We tried this and it was surprising how her whole family's health improved.

However, one day she appeared late and threw herself at my feet as I was preparing breakfast. Her face was white as flour; she stuck out her tongue which was bleeding red. She clung to her stomach and moaned; tears streamed down her face. She finally got half up and showed me how she was unable to straighten all the way, she was in such pain. She pointed to her wrists to indicate fever. All in all she was a sorry sight, and I couldn't get her out of the house quick enough. I felt sure she had some fatal malady. I told her to go immediately to the hospital. She staggered out and I, wondering if I should go along, rushed to watch her through the window.

No sooner had she closed the compound gate than she was walking sprightly down the *kutche*, straight as a rod, brushing the flour off her face with her *chador*.

TOO MANY COOKS

AFTER THREE WEEKS OF HOUSEKEEPING IN A STRANGE country, we had not become adjusted to all the frustrations, but we decided to go ahead with a dinner party for some of our newly made friends.

A cook had been suggested by an acquaintance. He was supposed to be the best, and although he had steady employment, Friday was his day off and he desired work on that day as a means of increasing his earnings. That's the day we set. His brother was a splendid waiter (so was said) and he, too, would come. Along with Eshra and her cousin, whom she had asked to be allowed to assist whenever possible, we felt we could manage.

As is customary, the cook was to do all the buying of the food. I had taken care of the details in my department and left the rest to him.

The morning of the party a messenger brought me word that the cook would be late. I took the message to my helpful Iranian neighbor who had attended the old American School, when it was in existence, and who spoke and read English. She translated that the cook would be later than we planned, but not to worry, he would be there.

If he was going to be as late as indicated, I decided

to have Eshra do the marketing. She could neither read nor write Persian, which was true of most all servants and the lower classes, and at this point I spoke very few words of it. However, with my trusty handbook, put out by the American Women's Club of Tehran, I figured out the names of everything I wanted and the quantities. We went over and over and over the order. She kept it all in her head as she had no other way of remembering, and assured me she knew it all perfectly. She said it back to me and it was all correct. Mohammed went for a taxi and I loaded Eshra, the mental instructions, and lots of rials (Iranian money) into it.

One hour passed, then three. I was becoming concerned. I had visions of her disappearing with the money. In my mind I began planning the steps I would take to have the party without food. Before I had been able to make a practical decision, I heard a car bumping up the *kutche*, a slamming on of brakes, then the gate bell. To say that I was relieved to see Eshra is putting it mildly. She came lugging sacks of things into the house. Mohammed followed, then his wife, and finally the taxi driver, all staggering under their loads. The stream of sacks and boxes kept coming. I followed into the kitchen and began peering into the containers. Food continued to arrive. We were running out of floor space. I became panicked. There was sack after sack of apples. I had planned to have a Waldorf salad, but not for the army. Spilling out of one box after another were tomatoes, dozens of them —finally hundreds of them, by the count. When all the activity had ceased, I stared at Eshra in bewilderment and realized that she had not understood.

She happily tied on her work apron after tossing off her *chador*, putting it to rest on a nail. She tumbled the fruits and vegetables onto the tile floor, picked them up by the handfuls to wash and soak as we always did. Since human fertilizer is used, it is necessary to take every precaution in cleaning all fresh vegetables. For this, our German friends preferred potassium permanganate, others used Roccal (says on the bottle, "Don't get near food") and although this evidently disinfected, it also made some people ill. Then there was perchlorine. After trying them all we lived happily by washing everything in Tide (detergent) and rinsing it carefully and thoroughly. To be really safe it was better to cook everything, and at least peel the fruits and vegetables which were to be eaten uncooked.

We ate everything, including the wonderful strawberries which vendors brought to our door every morning, fresh and fragrant in the summer. We used lettuce until Alice Morgan came by one day bearing a bleak and discouraging article on the hazards of eating lettuce in countries where human fertilizer is used. It stated that none of the above antiseptics would kill amoebic dysentery, and even fifteen or more years later the disease might crop out. We gave up the lettuce but not the strawberries, even though they were weary-looking and beaten to a pulp after being so womanhandled to make them safe. However, it was never the same as before that article, and I choked on every bite, delicious as it was. I had vague visions of myself lying fifteen years hence, on some sterile hospital bed taking the cure for amoebic dysentery. My anxiety was relieved when Mohammed took to raising strawberries and other fruits and vegetables in our garden in our own way.

In my usual Persian and charades I asked Eshra, "Why did you get so much? We can never use all of this. It is too much!" The communication penetrated and in like sign language she explained to me that I had said forty kilos (over eighty pounds) of apples and the same of tomatoes. She not only looked crestfallen but annoyed, then went on to explain it had taken her all that time to bargain and bargain and find everything I wanted, and now I complained. It wasn't easy, she added.

I ventured to explain that I said we were having forty people, not forty kilos. "*Balle, balle, balle* (yes, yes, yes)," she reiterated with authority and indicated I didn't know what I was talking about because I said forty kilos, and that was that!

It was then I knew I must spend more time learning Persian. But imagine my chagrin after doing just that to find out Eshra was Turkish, from Tabriz on the Turkish border, and spoke no more Persian than I. As long as she was with us our communication ran the gamut of pantomime. I don't care to be challenged but I think I am now expert in this art.

Lloyd's favorite entertainment was standing quietly in the shadows watching me try to explain something to the servants. He would then go into a hilarious take-off. If I were half as funny as he, I am wasting my time. Comedy is for me.

In order to make room for us in the kitchen I gave armloads of apples and tomatoes to Mohammed and Eshra. As our guests left the party that night each was given some of the same. Everyone thought it an unusual idea to present the guests with samples of food served and was sure the idea would catch on in Tehran.

The cook was to arrive at two in the afternoon. That hour passed, then three, four, five, and at five thirty his brother, Salahi, the waiter appeared. I was in a frenzy at this point because nothing had been done toward the meal. I had not gone ahead because the cook was bringing the meat. I sent Salahi at once to buy lamb roasts and we put them in the oven to cook as insurance. He assured me that his brother would arrive any minute and that he was such an expert cook he would have everything ready for any hour we wished to eat.

Six thirty came. "Where is your brother, Salahi? I can't wait any longer. Our guests will arrive any minute. I must have a cook!"

"He come, Madame, he come"—he looked frightened and hesitated—"me teenk, maybe he go girl friend."

I was shaken. "You mean maybe he has gone with his girl friend someplace? But you don't just go with girl friends in this country—not until you are married can you decently go out with a girl." I should tell them about their customs, but I hoped the cook was a good Moslem and it wasn't so. "He was here and we planned the menu. He knows he has to come to take care of lots of people. He has to come. You go get him!" I demanded.

"Me no find heem." Salahi shrugged. "Maybe he lost, no know how geet here."

"He was here yesterday. He knows how to get here." Salahi shrugged again.

"Are you sure he is coming? Is he dependable?"

"What ees defendable?"

"Oh, never mind. Do you know how to cook?" I was exasperated.

"*Balle*, me cook good."

"You do? Then get busy." I sat down with him and told him what we had planned for dinner. I put a knife in Eshra's hand and set her to peeling apples. I grabbed an apron and went to work. Eshra's cousin arrived and we gave her a job. The guests began coming. I wiped my sticky hands, took off the apron, and greeted each couple as they came. Between arrivals, I rushed to the kitchen to work and supervise.

Sherm would nervously appear at the door and wonder out loud why the cook didn't come.

"Stop talking about him and get busy and help. No, you take care of the guests and forget about the help. Give them these potato chips, crackers, and this stuff." I thrust some trays at him.

About eight o'clock things were shaping up. We would not have the original dinner, but we would have something. The cook had not appeared and he never did. It seems his employer got wind of the fact that he had another job and planned a dinner party herself for the same night. I didn't realize that the arrangement was unsatisfactory to her, because almost every Friday her cook was hired by some of my friends.

Mohammed came in after doing his job of "gate opener" to see if he could help. A gardener practically never enters a kitchen but Sherm had sent him. I was dumfounded to see him with a haircut, shave, full suit, and white bucks. The bucks are what got me. Usually he went barefoot or wore some quaint, antique rubber shoes for watering. His best were the regulation string shoes worn by the workmen and lower classes. He proved how much better Sherm was apparently doing with his Persian than I. There he stood, exactly as Sherm requested—and in Persian, too.

We had the dessert in hand as I had ordered cakes from the Point Four restaurant. Eshra had put the cart before the horse and the first thing had cut the cake and strewn forty dessert plates full of it over the kitchen floor. There is no counter space in a real Persian kitchen. All the work is done on the floor. We had improvised counter space, even boarding over the Persian stove for such, but there was not enough of it, and anyway the servants preferred to sit and squat on the floor the way they had done all their lives. I was the only one standing on my tired, aching feet. How I wished I had been raised a Persian, but somehow now I was too old to sit on the cold tile floor, especially in a tight brocade dress.

Extra dishes had been rented from one of the innumerable rental agencies where everything from spoons to chairs is obtainable. Oh, and neon and Christmas tree type lights in such an assortment of colors and shapes as is not to be found in the States. This is a big business in Tehran because wedding receptions and big parties are given by the hundreds, for thousands, by the upper-class wealthy Iranians. As I whipped in and out of the kitchen, I invariably and accidentally stepped on a few plates and broke them. When we came to settling our rental bill, we had to pay for most of what we had rented—they were demolished.

At nine o'clock I was able to circulate nonchalantly among the guests. Things were almost ready. It became a rule for us that when we entertained in Iran to expect the unexpected. Much more challenging that way! The lights frequently went out just as everyone arrived and stayed out the entire evening. This was what the teen-agers always hoped for, but it only seemed to happen to our staid old married crowd. And always just as we had run out of all but a few candles. The stumbling and confusion in the kitchen were bedlam at these times. The water heater blew up once during the main course. Without electricity the water pump can't work, so we would run out of water. Also, many a molded salad has disintegrated and refrigerator-made ice cream returned to slosh when the refrigeration went off with the electricity.

Ah, but we had one advantage over most of our friends. We had a gas range instead of the undependble kerosene ones. We had paid three times the price for it listed in the Sears catalogue, but it was worth it. Even though we were warned against butane, we knew we were smart enough to handle it.

The servants began putting food on the buffet table.

The Cook Didn't Come

I hurried to the kitchen to be sure the lamb roasts had not become cold. Sure enough, someone had turned off the oven, after I so carefully left it low to assure hot food. But not until the meat had been put on our two plastic trays and returned to it. What a sight greeted me as I thrust my head inside! The roasts and plastic had amalgamated into one horrible sticky mess. Somehow I controlled myself. It took strength I didn't know I had. But I did.

I was ready to announce to the guests that it was all a big joke and would they go home and come some other time. Then I thought of the two canned hams I had bought at the Commissary.

We got them in the oven to warm. I put the match to it. There was a wild, shattering boom. The next thing I knew my hair was on fire. I couldn't see. My ears were deaf. I couldn't move.

Marlene had just come in from an early dinner with a friend and was walking past the kitchen at this moment. She rushed in, saw my condition, beat out the flames around my face with a dish towel, and began screaming for Sherm.

Ali appeared as if by genii, which he always seemed to do when we were in trouble. He and Marlene led me to my bedroom. The dining room was too far away, along with the babble of voices, for anyone to hear. Ali quickly brought Sherm.

They told me afterward that the servants just stood there hugging the walls, in motionless terror, not making a move or sound.

I was stunned and sure that I was blind. I kept saying, "I can't see, I think it blew out my eyeballs."

"Try hard to open your eyes. Please try, dear," Sherm kept pleading. "If you can get them open then we will know."

Psychologically, I was afraid to open them for fear I really wouldn't be able to see.

Ali would whisper in the other ear, "You will see. Remember I am here, the son of Mohammed, and he wouldn't let you lose your sight with me here. You are all right. You will see—open them."

I opened them. I could see. Things were dim, but I could see Ali's white and immobile face, Marlene had tears streaming down hers, and Sherm was biting his lips.

"Oh, Mother, your poor hair all singed and no eyebrows and no eyelashes. But, don't worry, I'll take care of you." Marlene hugged me tightly.

After I blinked a few times, things began to clear. You know a woman's vanity. I had to see how I looked.

It wasn't pretty. No eyelashes, no eyebrows, and the entire front of my hair burned off, but at least there was evidently no permanent damage. That old reflex action had closed my eyes in time.

They insisted that I go to bed to recover from the shock but I didn't agree.

I sketched on eyebrows, combed out as much of the singed hair as possible and, smelling like a Hindu burial where they burn the body, went forth.

The first guests I encountered stared. I whispered, "The oven got a little out of control, but don't mention it to the others." I went from group to group with my explanation, and consequently no comment was made as each was keeping my secret.

Actually it turned out to be one of the gayest parties we ever had, one with the most fun. Not until the next morning did anyone comment on my appearance, then our *newly acquired* telephone began to ring and after "Hello," invariably a voice asked, "what happened?"

WRONG NAME, RIGHT FELLOW

AFTER A FEW DAYS' VACATION TRIP, WE RETURNED TO
find our garden bursting out all over with a profusion
of flowers and everything in and about the house in
perfect order, thanks to our faithful and dependable
Mohammed. Only thing missing was Eshra. She was
to have returned to work two days ahead of us, but
she hadn't shown up. We gave her a week, then decided to look for another servant. The day after we
had made up our minds to chalk Eshra up as a lost
cause, Salahi, the waiter, appeared with a young, beautiful girl wrapped fetchingly tight in a *chador*.

"Theese Eshra seester. She, you want *badji*," he announced.

"Well, fine thing. What happened to Eshra?"

"You no know? She say me tell. She wife number
two man now. He no want Eshra work. She send
seester."

This was a revelation. Eshra, who spent her spare
time, and most of the time she should have been working, regaling me about what louses husbands were and
how she would never, *never* have another one, was now
sharing one with another wife.

The sister spoke no English, very little Persian, but
her Turkish was excellent. I don't know a word of

Turkish. We decided to give her a try and I worked out our own confused communication system such as I had with Eshra. It was an enigma to everyone but the two of us.

Motara was an exquisite girl. She had a lighter skin than most of the peasant class, enormous, expressive, brown eyes, perfect white teeth, dimples, and a captivating smile. She had a lovely little girl of about two years. She told me her husband treated her miserably, then finally divorced her, she claimed, because she had a baby girl instead of a boy.

In the mornings she arrived without make-up, looking fresh and demure, but when she left in the evenings she looked as if she were ready and waiting for the "on stage" sign to light up. As she bid us good night she would flutter her heavily mascaraed eyelashes flirtatiously at the men of the family, using her *chador* for this purpose as she might have used a fan. There was *something* to be said for a *chador*.

I had bought uniforms for Eshra and now for Motara. The only way I could persuade either one to wear them was by explaining that it would be a saving on their other dresses. Motara could be inveigled into wearing her white uniform for all guests except Iranians. If she got wind of the fact that Iranians were coming, she refused to wear it. Nothing I could say or do would get results. One day I insisted she wear the uniform and, if not, give me a good reason why not. Why not was a vivid and descriptive performance, complete with sweeping gestures from one end of the kitchen to the other, emphatic enough that I understood.

Iranian wives do not want their female servants to look attractive as it might be tempting to the husband. If she looked too pretty the Iranians would be suspicious of her. Then she launched into an expressive, intense pantomime of what happened to her at the last Iranian home at which she had worked.

One day she wore a clean dress and looked rather nice, then (making her point with a combination of Turkish and Persian invectives) she showed me that Madame hit her hard all over. Then, in the only outburst of broken English she ever uttered in our home, she hollered, "Madame say God damn," and Motara continued to slap and beat herself furiously to show me Madame had meant business.

We saved the uniforms to wear for foreigners.

She was neat and a good housekeeper. However, like Eshra, she came only part of the time, using all sorts of excuses about sick relatives. I usually fell for them or, let's say, I was just too softhearted. I wanted someone more dependable so I gladly took the cook (and all-around houseboy) offered me by American friends who were leaving, and found Motara another job closer to her home and sick relatives.

It had been my wish to get along with as few servants as possible, since our family likes privacy. Usually, Americans have fewer servants than other foreigners and Iranians. Upper-class Iranians have many, all over the place. They are often retainers and considered part of the family. Some are born in the family, others are brought from the employer's villages. The servants are so specialized they can usually do but one type of work. One can serve tea, one can clean, one can cook and nothing else. However, it had been my dream to get all of these in one package. That is what I hoped I was getting when we got Doran.

He was among the elite top handful of servants who got the highest wages in Tehran. Because he was honest, always on time, and had no sick relatives, he was worth it, not because of his ability, and *certainly* not his intelligence. When he first came to us his name was Davood, and when he left it was Doran.

This change of name came about after he had been with us for about two months. Our good friends, the McCanns, called for us one day to take us to a barbecue, along with our barbecue equipment. They brought their cook to carry it. When their cook, whose name was also Davood, came face to face with ours, there was a great to-do. The two Davoods were waving their arms and screaming at one another. Sherm and Mike McCann had to intervene, and finally they got the McCann's Davood back into the car and we drove off.

The gist of their life stories, as translated to us, was that they were brothers. They had the same father but different mothers. The father had insisted that the McCann's Davood lend his letter of recommendation to our cook (years back) since ours was younger and had never worked. He had landed a job with an American family on the strength of that letter, and had been going strong as Davood ever since. When we returned home, our cook confirmed the story, admitting his name was really Doran. He and his brother had the fracas because the brother had been hiding out, trying to escape paying his share for the keep of the senile father.

He added that there were four brothers and it didn't really matter what we called him as their names were similar, so he didn't feel he had done much wrong by trafficking on his brother's name. The four brothers' names were Doran, Davood, Darop, and Davaad. In haste, in exasperation, and when we couldn't remember just which one, we ran the gamut of names.

Doran stayed with us until we left. Like most servants, he felt the Madame knew nothing about keeping house or a kitchen, especially cooking. It is true Iranian women leave most of this to the servants and many wouldn't be able to cook anything, even in a pinch.

Though it would end in a tug of war of ideas, I occasionally tried to assert myself and show him how to cook a new dish. It didn't matter that he had never seen or heard of the concoction before, the minute my back was turned something would be added (Sherm insisted it was always some kind of perfume). When the food arrived at mealtime, it had no resemblance to what I had left him stirring in the kitchen. He was stubborn and set in his ways and thought he knew everything. If I asked him to cook something in a certain manner there was always an argument that I was wrong because he never did it that way. Since Iranians boil chicken, he said that was the right and only way to cook chicken. The only time we ever had fried chicken was on his day off. This went for all the other food —we had it his way or not at all.

None of the others learned to handle the drip-dry

washing and neither did he. I went through the entire process countless times in front of him. I would
wash, then hang up the garment, without wringing,
and stress there was to be absolutely no wringing. As
many times as I did this, it was of no avail. I had Ali
explain this new material and the process, but Doran
would follow my instructions up to a point, then he
would madly wring the garment with all his strength
so that it was almost beyond saving, even with a good
ironing. He told Ali that everybody knows you always
wring out clothes when you wash them, and Madame
was crazy. Madame always had to launder these labor-
saving articles.

Doran thought he could speak English. He only
understood what we didn't want him to and little of
what we hoped he would. He could speak a few words,
like a parrot, which gave the false impression that he
really could speak and understand. Instead of "yes"
he said "Yezwa," and to show he understood (which
he seldom did), "Ees good."

Marketing is part of a cook's job, but I was not to
be saved this chore. No matter what I asked Doran
to buy, he would refuse and say, "Too much rials."
I would explain that it was our money and he was to
buy what I asked. He would go to the bazaar and
more often than not come back empty-handed, saying
everything was "too much rials." Sometimes I would
be able to badger him into getting a few wormy apples,
tired eggplant, or culls of one thing and another. They
weren't too much rials.

As a rule we would get—at least—one surprise at

each guest dinner. One night I had meticulously gone over everything. I had planned to have apple pie à la mode. I knew this would take a lot of explaining. We discussed apple pie for a while. He had said that "Yezwa," he would make apple pie. He had made ice cream in the refrigerator many times. "Yezwa," he would make ice cream.

"You remember the ice cream we had last week for guests and you served it in these sherbet glasses?" I went to the cupboard and brought out the glasses.

"Yezwa, yezwa," he said.

"Good, then you know what ice cream is. Tonight we are going to put the piece of pie on the plate." I showed him the plate on which the pie was to be placed. "Then, by the side of this we will put the ice cream—the pie and ice cream on this very same plate." I took the ice cream scooper and pantomimed the whole thing.

"Yezwa, yezwa. Ees good, ees good," and he gave me a disgusted look which meant, "Why do you keep on explaining."

Things had gone very well for a change at dinner until we came to the dessert. My back was to the door of the dining room, but as I heard Doran enter I saw by the expressions on our guests' faces that something was amiss. I turned to behold him straining, walking as if on eggs, slightly swaying, trying to balance the ice cream in the sherbet glasses, on top of the pie, all on a tray.

During the day we allowed him to use our radio in the kitchen. This gave him something else to do be-

Pie à la Mode

sides sitting on the stool and staring. Whenever I ventured past after a news broadcast he would jump to the door and say "Bang-bang Iraq," or "Lebanon," or some Middle Eastern neighbor. Something distressing went on throughout the entire two years we were there. Always some border trouble with somebody— disturbances in Egypt and Syria, the coup in Lebanon, the one in Iraq, the counterrevolutionary attempts, so the "banging" went on perpetually. I never failed to understand "bang, bang," but I often misunderstood in which country and frequently hauled out my evacuation bag, thinking it was Iran.

One day, as they do so often here, friends dropped in for tea, and as we were chatting amiably, Doran appeared, lugging our washing machine. He heaved it with great effort into the living room and clattered it down in the middle of the floor then just stood there. I must admit this annoyed me.

"Doran, what is the meaning of this? What do you want?"

"Machine no good. Finish, no good."

"Take it away, put it back where it belongs. We can't do anything about it now."

"Me, heem say, heem Madame say," he pointed to the one Iranian guest among them and began a lengthy and spirited discourse on why it was "finish."

The men began to make suggestions as to what was wrong with it and how it could be fixed. Sherm dismissed the whole thing by saying he would take it to a repair shop next morning and we would forget about it for the time being.

We had a self-styled mechanic in the group and nothing would do but he would fix it. Wouldn't take a minute. Doran hauled out all the screw drivers and tools he could scrape up in our house and in Mohammed's quarters. Our guest quickly took it apart. The putting-together process took much longer. One of the other men, who also felt he was a talented fix-it man, got into the act. After two hours they departed, leaving the machine just where Doran had plunked it, explaining if they only had enough time and a welding torch they could fix it, but under the circumstances perhaps it would be better if Sherm took it to the repair shop.

Next morning he loaded it into the car but, to my surprise, returned with it that evening in the same sad condition. One of the professors noticed it on the back seat of our car and said he repaired his own machine all the time—there was nothing to it, just a matter of tightening a couple of screws. He looked at it, said the agitator was stuck—simple. He worked away for some time when a mutual friend dropped in. The friend had another idea. After forty-five minutes of screwing and unscrewing things, I offered them tea. They retired to the living room and, wiping their brows, sat down to enjoy some refreshment. After this interlude it was almost dinnertime and both friends had a dinner engagement.

After a week, in the dark of night, Sherm, purposely making a detour around the university, got the machine to the repair shop. It took two more weeks to renovate the damages caused by the various "fix-it friends."

As I sat in my comfortable chair in Glendale, when we made plans for our journey, I had visualized the servants of Iran. I saw them in immaculate uniforms, even a butler with white gloves, and all the servants jumping to attention at the flick of Madame's finger. Once I arrived in Tehran this illusion was quickly dispelled. The most common *badji* outfit is some kind of long pants, pajama bottoms or what have you, hanging down beneath a worn and faded skirt, some kind of mismatching jacket (often a man's coat given by a former employer), and a scarf tied tightly over all the head. When she steps out of the house a *chador* is thrown on over all this. Female servants from the provinces wear the costume popular in that region. One of our friends had two *badjis* who wore a type of white fish net over their heads which dangled annoyingly in the food and got caught on the beads of our dinner dresses as they served.

Then there was the Morgan's houseboy who wore an antique GI hat with the bill turned up, a dirty white apron, and ancient gray sweat pants with holes in the most unbecoming part of the exterior. Nothing could make him remove his hat. We suspected he must be bald.

Ali had one servant who, all during the winter, wore a heavy, delapidated overcoat while serving. Knowing Ali well enough, I asked him, "Why?"

"Says he is cold," Ali reported to me.

"Can't think of a better reason," I agreed.

With one revolution after another raging in the countries around us, we thought the time might come when the loyalty of our servants could be sorely tested if our lives were endangered. Opinion was divided on what to expect. Some Iranian friends told us the servants would stand by and help; others said they would be the first to knife us (a comforting thought!). I am glad the showdown never came. Somehow we felt Mohammed (our gardener) would stand by us. He lived in the compound with his little family of one wife, two-year-old son Reza, and another—they hoped —boy on the way. They came with the house.

When Sherm was gone on hunting trips and I was home alone, the little family would all three sleep outside my door. Whenever we returned in the night from a journey there we would find faithful Mohammed on guard, asleep on the floor outside our bedroom door.

In the spring, summer, and autumn we ate most of our meals on our upper terrace overlooking the magnificent garden. When I am ninety I will still think lovingly of those wonderful days with the view and attention. At breakfast we could depend on Mohammed to emerge from nowhere and present us, with a flourish, either a colorful bouquet of his well-tended flowers, or strawberries, cherries, or vegetables he grew in the garden at the far end of our compound.

I had hoped Mohammed's wife would be able to have her second baby in the spring. I was afraid their quarters wouldn't be comfortably warm in winter. One day, as the last snow was disappearing from the mountains just behind us, I returned from an exhilarating walk to find Doran in the kitchen behind a haze of steam.

"What is the matter?" I asked.

"Too much water. Mohammed's baby come. Ees good."

I saw pans full of water all over the stove, steaming away.

"Is Mohammed's wife going to have her baby—now —today, this very minute?" I was excited.

"Me no know. Ees good. Maybe today, maybe *farda* (tomorrow). Mohammed he me say *abe jus* (hot water)."

I knocked on the gardener's door. Mohammed finally got the message over to me that his wife had been in labor for four hours and was having a bad time of it. She had lost two other babies and maybe would lose this one. He had brought a midwife but she didn't know what to do—so she left. Mohammed was going now to find another midwife. I noticed several ladies standing in the room hovering over the wife. When I asked who they were I was told they were the wife's mother, two sisters, and a sister-in-law come to assist.

At least I would be relieved of Alice's experience of having to sit in until the bitter end when her houseboy's wife had a baby and Alice all but had to deliver it. The houseboy arrived with the midwife at the same time the baby was arriving. I was glad to see those women in attendance.

Now and then I would press my ear to Mohammed's door, but never did I hear any violent moaning—just a low wail. I kept sending Doran to ask if they were ready for the water. After five hours of this I wondered how the poor mother-to-be was holding up. I was quite exhausted myself.

Mohammed called to Doran to bring the hot water, and it was not too long before our faithful gardener appeared at our back door to announce he was the proud father of a second son. There is no greater blessing to these people than sons.

We waited for what we thought was a decent interval, then went to offer congratulations. Into the small room we stepped to find fourteen people bedded down on the floor for the night. "Relatives," Mohammed said.

There lay the mother, spent and perspiring with son Reza cuddled up beside her. We didn't see the baby, but at our inquiry as to where it was, one of the visiting women plucked it from among the blankets and handed it to me.

The little red-faced thing was tightly wrapped from neck to feet and looked like a tiny mummy which could surely stand by itself for hours with all those wrappings to bolster it. I had heard of swaddling clothes but never had seen anything really swaddled before. It was a cinch we would never have to worry about hearing him cry as it would have been impossible for him to move enough to get that much breath into his lungs.

After we duly admired the baby, Mohammed told us that Reza was very jealous. When they told him he had a new baby brother he said our equivalent of, "Take it away. I don't want it. Get it out of here," and proceeded to demonstrate by pushing it out the door and hitting at it. Human emotions seem to be the same in every culture!

When we got back into the house I asked Doran, "Were your babies all wrapped up like that after they were born?"

"Yezwa."

"For how long?"

"Long time—me teenk—year—one."

"Why do you wrap them?"

"Make legs, arms make —" then he gestured — "straight."

Sherm turned to me. "Can't you get someone to explain to Mohammed's wife that a baby needs to exercise and use its legs and arms?"

"Are you kidding? After the thousands of years they have been doing this sort of thing, I should make suggestions. They wouldn't believe me anyway. Who am I to tamper with their beliefs? If they did unwind him, it would just be my luck to have him turn out to be permanently bowlegged. I'm not going to cast a spell or put my evil eye on him. Not me! After all, we have bright blue beads hanging in our house to ward off just that kind of calamity."

Doran kept showing us how the baby would have crooked legs if they didn't keep them bound straight.

Swaddling clothes are often used instead of diapers. They don't change the babies as often as we do—just a few times a day whether they need it or not—but not just when they need it.

For three days the gay group of people stayed on, drank tea, and visited.

Ali happened by with a silver tray filled with dates from his village for us, so we buttonholed him and got him to go with us to Mohammed's quarters and find out more about the people and baby.

"I would love to know why all those people keep staying. That poor mother needs rest," I said.

"It is traditional among this class of people to have all the family who live within a reasonable distance come to visit right after the baby is born. Some of them will be going home, but the grandmother or sisters or someone will stay for ten days until they take the baby to the bath," Ali told us.

Ali went in and offered congratulations. He really liked Mohammed, particularly because he had come from Ali's section of the country, Fars. To have such an important personage as Ali, who was well known, come to visit them in their humble quarters was a great event.

Reza began to yowl when we paid attention to the baby, so Ali picked him up and tried to comfort him. He took out a handful of coins and gave them to the child. Reza only howled louder, so Ali kept filling his palms with money. Mohammed all but strangled the child to shut him up in front of us and Ali, but Reza was unimpressed with our importance and cried the whole time as we shouted over the wailing.

Ali has a big, soft heart. He looked around the room and began passing out money to each guest. He gave a special amount to the new mother and father and only left after giving away every rial from a recently cashed, sizable check. This was Ali, impetuous and sensitive, with deep understanding and affection for those less fortunate than he.

SLEEPWALKERS

My first visit to the University of Tehran came at examination time. Ali had been commandeered by Sherm to take me there for my first reception at the beautiful University Club. Poor man, we didn't realize at that time what a strain it must put him under to be seen in public at his old alma mater, and also where he taught, in the company of a woman to whom he wasn't married and, worse still, someone else's wife. Well, ignorance is bliss and happily I went along.

Ali's driver was at the wheel this day and he drove us through the heavily guarded gates, past Reza Shah's statue, and stopped in front of the Law Faculty Building.

The main campus was completely surrounded by a tall iron-post fence, with two entrances guarded by blue-coated attendants. A road bordered by the season's flowers circled the inner quad of the campus with the main buildings all fronting on this quadrangle. A large modern mosque had been under construction for two years in the very center of the campus.

"Say, was that the new gym way over to the side at the left as we came in?" I asked.

"That new building?" asked Ali.

"Yes. It's a much better gymnasium than most of

the colleges in the States have. I enjoyed that basket-
ball game between the Turkish team and the Iranian
one. I was shouting my head off for the Iranians.
You know, I understood everything they said. You
will laugh at this but I said to Sherm in the middle of
it, 'It's amazing how well I understand Persian and for
being here such a short time. I understand every word
that referee has said.' Sherm said, 'Well, you should
be able to, it's all in English!' "

Ali laughed. "Can't even distinguish between the
two languages now, huh? They had to have a common language so the boys could understand."

"Those girl gymnasts were excellent. How come you
allow women to get out and perform like that?"

"This is a recent development. It isn't looked down
upon so much now, although it isn't entirely accepted
by any matter of means. The Shah likes to see girls
develop their bodies and become strong. He is athletic
himself and encourages this."

"I'm all for it. Think it's a good thing."

"We better go." Ali hopped out.

I stepped out and immediately came face to face
with a crowd of students pacing up and down, back
and forth, books in hand, some mumbling aloud, others
with lips moving silently. I had never seen anything
like it. My mind began darting back to all the student trouble of the past, especially to the time the Shah
was shot in the jaw in 1949 while entering the law
school—and at this very point, right here—where he
had come to attend a university anniversary celebration.

Naturally, I was startled and backed up.

"What's the matter?" Ali inquired.

"Maybe we better not go in. Are they preparing for some kind of demonstration or something?"

"They are just preparing for their examinations." He smiled.

"Why aren't they home studying then?"

Ali seemed surprised at my reaction. "Why, they always study like this. More today because of examinations. It's the custom. They are memorizing. You will see we even build our buildings with more space for halls than classrooms so the students will have more room to walk."

"Good heavens, how can they concentrate with so much confusion! How do they keep from bumping into one another?" I inquired.

"They don't always. This is the way we memorize. We have done it like this for a long time. Our entire educational system is based on memory."

It was always the same thereafter when I went to the university, only to a lesser degree than at examination time. It was also a common sight to see students pacing around and around a street light on park walks, meditating and memorizing, or moving along the main streets in the evenings.

We made it into the main hall where we came upon another throng of students doing the same thing with measured and unvarying steps. They would march to the end of the hall, make an about face without looking up, and start back again. We pushed in and out and made it to the stairway with students glancing occasionally at me, mainly because I am a foreign woman and because there are only 5 per cent of my sex in attendance at the university. Sherm was waiting in his office.

I took a quick look around. "How do you like it?" Sherm asked.

"Very nice, but before we go to the reception I have a lot of questions on my mind. Dr. Azizi, tell me about the university. Has it been here quite a while?"

"It's relatively new. Reza Shah founded it in 1934 under a special act of the Majlis. He thought he would Westernize and modernize Iran through it. He copied it from the methods used in France."

"Then I suppose the professor is the law and final word, the way it is in the French schools?"

"Obedience to authority is the entire guiding motif of education in Iran."

"You mean the student is not supposed to think for himself?"

"That's about right. You see there are few textbooks written in Persian, so the professor becomes the sole authority in his special field. All the basic information has to come, of necessity, from the instructor. The student memorizes everything he gets from the lectures, and by taking careful notes, then on examination day he pours it all out to the professor again."

Sherm injected, "Some of the professors were telling me yesterday that often they will draw a question from a hat. If the student fails to answer that one question he flunks the exam—and the course—and has to take his entire year over again, not just the course. That makes it tough."

"You just don't know how important that diploma

is," added Ali. "People will do anything to get a paper of some kind, some certificate to show they have been to an educational institution. We have a proverb which, translated into English, is 'Those who know are strong,' which to you means 'Knowledge is strength.' We believe that."

"What about all the political activity I read about at the time of the Mossadegh trouble? Sounded as if this place is a hotbed of student political demonstrations."

Ali was quick to speak. "You will find we are a very individualistic people. We are not shy about expressing our ideas. Like me for instance." He grinned.

We had already had many rather warm international political arguments with him. I knew what he meant.

"I was—what you say—active—yes—pretty active myself in my undergraduate days about what I thought was right for my people. But I don't want to get started on that."

Sherm nodded at this and suddenly changed the subject. "Say, I'm impressed at the great prestige of college professors here. Certainly different from the States. When I walked into our class they stood up in unison at stiff attention until I waved them to be seated. A few came late but stopped, bowed, apologized profusely before taking their seats. We could use some of this back home."

"A professor here carries the highest prestige in the country. Most of the outstanding ones, with the right family connections, receive appointments to the Senate or other positions of importance. Some professors hold six or eight outside jobs. They are assigned only one class a day and no campus activities, so that isn't hard. That's why I asked you to introduce me as a professor instead of a judge—remember—I asked you to do that?"

"And I thought I was giving you more prestige by calling you 'Judge,' " Sherm said.

"Another thing I want to know: is your education compulsory?"

"The schools for the most part are state schools and the primary grades are compulsory by law, but it's pretty hard to make it stick. We don't have enough teachers or buildings in the first place."

"How does a student get to the secondary schools?" I wanted to get all the information I could while I had a chance.

"When a kid is twelve he is given an exam and if he can pass then he is entitled to enter high school. The majority can't afford to continue. They have to help earn the family bread, so they become apprentices or whatever they can find to do. There is a law against young kids working but we still have the child sweat-shops as you used to have in your country. They exist especially in Isfahan, Shiraz, and the villages. The government tries, but they seem to have some kind of —clever—what is it you say?—uh—ingenious system for hiding the kids when an inspector shows up. Another proverb we have is, 'There are lots of knots in the judge's house,' which means, 'Don't worry, that's none of your business.' Many authorities take this attitude."

"Just one or two more questions," I begged. "Do you mind?"

"Go ahead. Get it off your mind. We have time. Don't want to be first ones there, anyway," Ali assured me.

"Once you struggle through the secondary schools here, then can you get into the university?"

"I only wish it were that easy—just get in. No. A final exam is given after the sixth year of high school. If you pass this you get another thrown at you. From all the thousands who apply, only a few make the grade. Take the engineering school over there." He waved his hand at a building. "Two thousand applied, and two hundred were taken. Of these two hundred, 30 per cent are dropped at the end of the first year, another 30 per cent at the end of the second. Pretty rough."

Sherm nodded. "I'm told that family connections play a big part in getting some students in—as well as out—and into good jobs."

"Uh-huh, you can't underestimate family here. In most things it counts for more than any other single factor. However, sometimes the family gets the boy in, but he would have to have some pretty powerful connections to keep him in if he is flunking," Ali said.

"Time to go." Sherm looked at his watch a second time and jumped up.

As we walked through the building Ali explained, "The law school is the oldest with the most prestige, I'd say. It's been operating in its present form for twenty years. It is the only law school in Iran. Last year only two hundred out of one thousand five hundred applicants were admitted. Depends on space avail-

able. Lots of important leaders of this country have
come through these doors. In all the schools of the
university we have altogether around ninety-five hundred students. You see, this takes care of only a frac-
tion of the students who want to come."

As we went along and I observed the buildings it
was apparent that they were built for grandeur with
those massive, enormous hallways—and—oh, yes, for
the memorizing students.

We followed the crowd to the University Club which
is the center of social activity. There were a pool and
fountains, surrounded by the inevitable gardens. Inside were two big banquet rooms with plush decorations and costly chandeliers. Many of our most pleasant hours in Iran were spent attending receptions here
as guests of the hospitable Iranian professors.

HALF THE WORLD

IN A TORRENTIAL DOWNPOUR THE STATION WAGON skidded to a slushing, muddy halt crosswise in front of our gate. It was a matter of providence that it did not disappear completely into one of the mammoth holes in our *kutche*.

Alice and Bill Morgan, their twelve-year-old daughter and eight-year-old son, along with Marlene, Sherm, and me, were going to fly to Isfahan (the heart of Persia) that morning.

"Certainly they won't fly in this weather," Sherm commented as he, Bill, and the driver slipped around in the mire trying to get the car going in the right direction.

"Probably will. Better go to the airport and check in anyway. Hope you like adventure," replied Bill.

We huddled together in the unheated airport. "Here it is, only five thirty in the morning, and the plane doesn't leave until seven," Alice grumbled. "Why did you get us up so early?"

"I'm afraid to fly in this storm. It's crazy." Marlene popped up her head.

"I think so, too," I agreed, "but either they won't fly, or it will let up—one or the other."

At a quarter after six they were ushering us onto the Iranian Airways plane.

"But it doesn't leave until seven," I protested. "Why do we have to board forty-five minutes early?"

"Yes, why?" asked Alice.

"My dear, they are ready to take off," said Bill. "They're revving the motors right now. If you want to go, you better hurry."

It was still raining, but lightly now. However, none of us had much heart for the flight.

Suddenly Sherm spun around. "Ali isn't here! What can we do? Bill, let's see if we can get them to hold the plane. He will be here when it is supposed to leave."

"You can try, but it won't do you any good," said Bill resignedly.

"They can't do that—leave so far ahead of schedule. Why, never heard of such a thing," Sherm fumed.

"They can't do it, but they do—all the time," stated Bill, who had lived in Persia long enough to know whereof he spoke. "They are famous for taking off too early or way late. Don't have an accurate passenger list in the first place, so they leave whenever they feel like it, whether the passengers are here or not." Bill squeezed into a seat. "May as well sit down and relax."

"But Ali will have missed the entire trip. Poor us. We can't accomplish anything without him to interpret and show us around. He has made all the arrangements for visiting the factories." Sherm wouldn't give up.

Sherm began pleading with the stewardess, who re-

referred him to the copilot, who told him they were taking off as of now and—that was that!

For an hour we clutched at the arms of our seats as our DC-3 was tossed around like a fluttering leaf. Under the most favorable conditions it's a rough trip, hedgehopping over the high mountains. The dramamine we had consumed became totally ineffective. We all fell silent and stoical. We placed our fate in the hands of Allah.

In the last fifteen minutes of flight we broke out of the storm into rays of brilliant sunlight playing on that ancient city of Isfahan, referred to in Persian proverbs as "Half the World."

There it lay below—an oasis of green, fertile valley with its slender poplars flashing in the sun, its bright river spreading out into countless irrigation ditches. Most magnificent of all were the blue tile domes and graceful minarets of the mosques.

Bill, considering himself an authority on anthropology and the history of Iran, informed us that from 1051 the history of Isfahan really begins. "You know, when Seljuk Turks swept over the whole Middle East, they established an empire stretching from India to the Mediterranean, making Isfahan their capital. Very few traces left of its previous history. One is the fire temple of the Zoroastrians (Parsees) just out of the city. We will see it."

We did see this isolated temple built on a hill, which was the usual way it was done in those days. A circular stone structure was the inner sanctuary, where the sacred flame to Ahura-Mazda (their name for God) was kept burning year in and year out.

"Say, we must have got our name for Mazda lamps and light bulbs from them. Do you suppose?" Marlene asked.

"Must be. I don't know of any other Mazdas," I answered.

All Iranians were Zoroastrians until the Arab conquest (beginning in A.D. 630). Their prophet was Zoroaster, who transformed the primitive religion of the Aryan peoples into a lofty religion of the struggle between good and evil, between the one god they worshipped, Ahura-Mazda, the god of Light and Wisdom, and Ahri, the Power of Darkness.

Bill told us they believe in man's ability to shape his own destiny, as opposed to the Moslem concept of fate willed by Allah. Zoroastrianism was established in the sixth century B.C. as the state religion of the Persian Empire, then it was restored by the Sassanian Dynasty, but only to be overthrown by the Arabs in favor of Islam in the seventh century A.D.

He went on to say, "It is primarily an agricultural religion, having grown out of the early Persians' awareness of the supernatural in the performance of their daily tasks. They call their holy book the Zend-Avesta. It deals directly with the care of crops and animals as well as with the soul. To them, earth, air, fire, and water are the sacred elements. Fire and sun are their symbols of faith. As you know the sun is part of the Persian royal emblem today.

"When I studied Comparative Religions, I was fascinated enough with their burial practices that I always remembered they were the believers who dressed the deceased in their best finery and jewels, and left them in the open to be devoured by vultures."

Today this has become impractical in Iran (although one of these burial grounds still stands just outside of Tehran). The bodies are put in caskets.

"Good thought, good work, and good deed," is the motto of Zoroastrianism. It is an optimistic faith in that good will overpower the spirit of evil in time. They do not proselytize. At present there are about 16,000 or 17,000 in Iran. They are renowned for their honesty, skill, and success. This prestige has been maintained throughout the centuries. It has even accompanied them to India, where they form, particularly in Bombay, a wealthy and highly respected community of about 110,000.

The religion was restored to official favor by Reza Shah, as he turned to past history for inspiration for his regime.

In thinking back over the past few months, I recalled that our Zoroastrian friends are some of the most admirable people in all of Iran. They are highly respected in Tehran, and it is with reverence and respect that even a Moslem will say, "He is a Zoroastrian," which is the highest compliment for honesty and integrity.

As one of our Zoroastrian friends said, "Our big problem at present is that we do not take in new blood. We must marry within our religion, and now we are becoming much too inbred."

Ali appeared in the hotel dining room as we were having tea. "I made it on my magic carpet. Fine thing, you going off without me! Why did you let them do it?" he asked petulantly.

All at once, one trying to outshout the other, we explained that we had no control over the operation of Iranian Airways, unfortunately. He smiled good-naturedly. "Ah, the stupid—well, I finally got the next plane out and, believe me, I was there in plenty of time—four hours!"

"Sit down and have some tea," we said.

"O.K., but we can't take too long because I have appointments for you all the rest of the day."

Isfahan is the home of silver, copper, and enamel-ware production, among other industries, and Sherm had come to make a study of these in particular. Ali hustled us out, and we began the rounds.

Most of the work is done in small shops or fronts of homes. Little fellows can be seen sitting on the cold, dirt floor, pumping a bellows, painting a plate, carving a dish, grinding some powder, or sawing camel bone to be used for cigarette or jewelry boxes.

"They are back where we were in the old child-labor sweatshop days," Bill remarked. "However, I think this has merit. These are families working together. Each child has a job in which he takes pride and he is learning; it brings the family closer, keeps the children off the streets and from becoming delinquents."

"I agree with you," I said emphatically. "Maybe we have moved too far in the other direction. We can

certainly take a lesson in the child-delinquency department from Iran. There is no bloodthirsty delinquency
here as we know it in the States."

"You're right," Ali chimed with definiteness, his
patriotism showing through. "Now for the big treat.
I'm going to let you walk around the Great Imperial
Square," he said as we came out of the dingy little
shop with the din of the hammering of copper trays
still ringing in our ears.

"Now—everybody stand still and look—just look.
Isn't it magnificent?"

"Why, it's positively enormous!" Marlene rhapso-
dized.

Ali continued, "They say it used to be the biggest
in the world, and now that it is second in size only to
the Red Square in Moscow—some still say this is big-
ger. You have heard of old Shah Abbas. He was the
one who moved his capital here and made a new city.
He was the guy who started the whole business here."

"I know when it was, too—1598. Just read it a few
minutes ago in the guidebook," I said triumphantly.

The square was built for a concourse and parade
ground. Polo was first played in Persia. Many of the
famous Persian miniatures depict the polo games in
this square.

"Oh, look—everybody look—can you see—the goal
posts are still standing. Isn't that unbelievable?" I
shrieked.

"Yeah, I know. Takes you back a *long* time ago
when you played on the women's polo team for South-

ern California, I suppose." Sherm waited for me to
dispute the "long" but I let him have his inning.

The square is ringed with the palace, Imperial Mosque,
palaces and pavilions of nobles, and spacious, enchant-
ing gardens of colorful flowers.

"Some people wanted to build apartment houses here
but they finally decided against it," said Ali.

"That would have been a shame," Sherm observed.

I had read that under Shah Abbas the textile and
carpet weaving reached almost incredible perfection.
Great carpets woven in the royal workshop and destined for palaces or shrines were fabulously expensive
to produce. As I saw them hung on the walls of the
museums, I couldn't believe that such priceless objects
were actually made to walk upon.

The patterns on the carpets were similar to what
they weave today. They were of nature—the flowering garden, hunting scenes, animals, fields with rows
of flower-filled vases, and all-over foliage designs. The
earliest preserved carpets, which have great distinction,
date from the opening of the sixteenth century. This
craft remained at its peak throughout the entire hundred years. In the most luxurious of all, Polonaise carpets, the patterns are interwoven with silver and gilded
threads.

Never before had I been able to appreciate fully a
Persian rug. Now that I had been shown how long
it takes to make them and the intricacy of the art,
I shall never fail to admire them.

Secrets of dyeing account for the unrivaled beauty
and durability of these rugs. The process of extract-

ing vegetable dyes is guarded closely and handed down from father to son. Many colors have been lost, as the families became extinct. It has not been possible to duplicate certain colors which these dyers produce with very simple ingredients. Each dyer seems to have some peculiar and secret method of producing certain shades. Colors have a great significance to the weavers. Blue symbolizes air; red, joy; green, a sacred color to the Moslem, stands for immortality; black, sorrow or evil.

An expert can distinguish between chemical and vegetable dyed rugs by feeling them. Chemical dye robs the wool of its oil, which makes it stiffer, harder, and drier. The old-fashioned, meticulous rugmaker usually refuses to work with chemically dyed wools even though vegetable dyes require much more involved preparation. The old rugs colored with vegetable dyes contain subtler tones than the modern ones steeped with synthetic dyes.

The quality depends upon design, number of knots per square meter, and the grade of wool and dye used. Americans prefer rugs with a high pile, although this prohibits small stitches since the wool is thick.

The most popular way of having them cleaned is in the famous waters of Rey, a town on the outskirts of Tehran. There is supposed to be a certain chemical in a stream at that village which gives them special luster. It is a fascinating sight to see the hundreds of rugs being washed there. After the rugs have been beaten with long poles, the men, barefooted, stamp on them in the stream and shake them out in the water, giving them a thorough working over. They are then stretched out on a hillside to dry. It's a breathtaking sight to see all those brilliantly colored rugs covering the hill and gleaming in the sun. There must be something to their faith in that water, because the rugs come out with shimmering brightness.

Ali took us for a leisurely walk around Isfahan's awe-insipiring square. We had so much to absorb that we began to feel tired and made a few complaints about wanting to rest.

"That's all right. If you are tired I will take you to my cousin's house for tea. He is the one I told you about who just got married to my cousin. They are both my cousins."

"Glad you have relatives wherever we go. Darned convenient for us," Sherm commented.

Cousin Kareem and his wife were most hospitable (as are all the Persians I have met). We were served many kinds of delicacies and cup after cup of tea, sherbet, and fruit juices. He brought out his recent wedding pictures and we all crowded round. There were a few other guests, and soon I noticed they were staring at Marlene and exchanging whispered comments.

Ali caught my quizzical look and came to interpret what they were saying.

"They are wondering if Marlene is married," he said.

"Married!" I exclaimed. "Why, she is only a child of sixteen. Of course not."

"That's the best age to marry here—that's our legal age. A very pretty girl is usually taken to be a wife before she gets much beyond sixteen. They are saying she is beautiful with big eyes, fair and rosy complexion, and a face like a moon. You see, over here, to compare a woman's face with the moon is the highest compliment we can give. So why is she not married? they say. They are confused." He shrugged.

"Oh, please do explain to them that our customs are different. She is too young to shoulder the responsibilities of marriage in our country. It will be up to her, anyway, because she will select her own mate. Then she will probably not have any servants, and she will hope that her mother-in-law won't run her home as is done here. She has to learn how to run a home and raise a family because there will be no one to do it for her."

Ali moved from group to group with the explanation. It was received with dubious headshakes and many comments.

"They just can't understand," he gesticulated with fervor. "They think your custom is no good. I told them when she is ready she will find her own husband. That shocked them! Did you see how they looked?" He laughed hilariously. Ali was such a jester, I wasn't sure he had not made his own additions when he explained us to them, but he swore on the Koran he had not.

"Good night, everybody." Ali bowed and shook our hands as he escorted us to our hotel rooms. "Tomorrow we see the rug weaving."

Next day as we entered the first factory Ali explained, "Rug factories are usually just a home with one, or maybe two looms." We went in.

"The loom is always on a raised platform like this one. See that old woman? She is the master weaver, the other three are her helpers."

"Say, this is great. They are making a pair of rugs. See, the looms are standing side by side. Want to get a picture of this." Sherm got out his camera and began shooting.

He photographed a pair of rugs approximately five by nine feet in size. They were only half completed and they had been in the making for a year and a half.

"The old lady says they would probably sell for— let me put it from toman into dollars—for—well, about $1,800 to $2,000 apiece. That's not too much. Some of the finer ones run about fifty dollars a square foot, or over $5,000 for a rug this size—what you say—?"

"Nine-by-twelve," I filled in.

Rugs are the Persians' bank account. Some of our wealthy friends had two and three layers on their floors, with the excess hung on the walls or doorways, and other surplus kept at Bank Melli (National Bank).

After a few rug factories, Marlene asked, "Now, where do we go?"

"Out here a few miles to New Julfa to see the Armenian settlement, but let's stop and eat some melons first. Have to have melon in Isfahan because it is noted for them."

"Doran, our cook, keeps telling me the best melons are from here. I think all the ones I have had in Tehran from all over Iran are excellent. I have been told that your climate is peculiarly adapted to raising them and that the flavor can't be duplicated anywhere else in the world," I contributed.

Ali smiled and gave me an affirmative nod as we walked along toward the little restaurant. He ordered four varieties for the eight of us. "In Iran we have twenty distinctive kinds, even watermelons. I don't think you have that many in the States," he observed.

"Just the minute melon season comes we start eating melons like crazy. Can't get enough of them, a great blood builder. In some villages where the water is bad, they can take its place."

At New Julfa we came upon a lovely little settlement which was dominated by a beautiful cathedral, only distinguishable from the mosques by the huge cross on top of the dome. "Shah Abbas brought the Armenians from Julfa, which is on the Caucasian border of Iran, by the thousands," said Ali.

"Why?" asked Marlene.

"He did it to save them from the Turks, who are notorious for their torture of them. Then, too, he wanted their fine craftsmanship for himself."

Sherm said, "You Persians are noted for your tolerance to other races and religions. It tells about it in the New Testament of our Bible, and all through history you read incidents of their kindly behavior toward defeated enemies. This was at a time, too, when barbaric cruelty was the rule. All the Armenian friends we have made here attest to this good treatment."

"Any foreigner is treated as a guest in our country," Ali proudly said.

"The Armenians have done well for Persia, too. They stimulated foreign and domestic trade. Even the court interpreters in Shah Abbas' time were Armenians."

TWO HUNDRED YEARS OF GLORY

THE NEXT MORNING WE LEFT THE FAMOUS BLUE-TILED domes of Isfahan behind as we hopped a plane for a two-and-a-half-hour ride to another ancient capital, the beautiful garden city of Shiraz, the former home of our Ali Azizi.

Since the Shirazi is considered to be the epitome of politeness and hospitality, even in Persia, our conversation focused on this trait as we were taken to our hotel from the airport.

Bill expounded, "Even in the seventeenth century, a visitor to this country wrote, 'The Persians are the most Civilized people of the East, and the greatest Complimenters in the world'!"

"Hasn't changed a bit," Marlene remarked.

"Everybody says the Shirazi is the most subtle, ingenious, vivacious, warmest and most happy-go-lucky of all his countrymen. His accent is supposed to be the most melodious. How about that?" asked Sherm. "Say, Ali, that description fits you like a glove. The guy who wrote that must know you."

Ali colored, then gave a self-conscious laugh. "I've been in Tehran for almost twenty years. Changed my accent to Tehrani and probably have grown out of that description."

Almost together we said, "Oh, no you haven't."

When a Persian greets you, and when he takes his leave, he always bows. The more distinguished you are the lower he bows, and puts his hand over his heart. Even the people who are forsaking the traditions and manners of the past begin conversations with such phrases as "This slave thinks" or "I am your sacrifice." In Persian "You and I" will become "This slave and your honor." This courteous repartee, before you get down to the subject, can go on for ten minutes or more and is called *taarof*.

"Do all Persians say all those flowery things, Ali?"

"It is our custom and it has become a habit just as you say 'How are you,' but you really don't care too much. We just naturally say these things even if we think the person is an old goat and hate him. We have a proverb, "Better a lie that gladdens the heart than a truth that saddens one.' However, your idea that we don't mean what we say is not really true. We consider a direct 'no' as impolite. That goes for business as well. It is better to say 'yes' and mean 'no' or 'maybe.' I know this is difficult for you to understand but you will get used to it."

Sherm said, "I know that a conversation as we understand it is a barbarism to Persian ears. We foreigners must be a distressing jolt to the ones who haven't been to the States and Europe!"

"One of my favorite remarks made by a Persian friend when I have entertained him and he leaves is often, *'Sayeh ye shoma kam, nashavad* (May your

shadow never become less).' What does that mean?" I
questioned.

"That saying was born from the hot burning desert
sands of Iran. When you stand in the sun you cast
a shadow. If your friend stands in the shadow he
finds protection. In other words, he hopes that your
influence will always be near."

As I said, "I like that," the jeep jerked to a halt.

The approach to our hotel, the Park Saadi, was most
inviting. In front was a pool, the size of a lake, which
reflected the flowers, trees, and shrubs of the surround-
ing gardens by day and the myriad colored lights by
night.

After delivering us safely there, Ali left our ranks
to stay with his oldest brother, who had become the
nominal head of the family with the recent death of
their esteemed father. This brother is a colonel in the
Iranian army and lives in the family home in Shiraz
in order to manage the Azizi villages of Fars.

After breakfast, next morning, Ali and his brother
came to insist that we all move to the colonel's home
for the rest of our stay.

They explained that it would be Persian fashion,
and we would sleep on the floor. We were really anxious
for the experience, and they were so persuasive that
we accepted.

Sharing their daily life proved to be the high light
of our visit in Shiraz. In the evenings there were
parties of distinguished friends who had been prominent in the country's leadership from the time of Reza
Shah, through Mossadegh, and up to the present. The

dining table was always heaped with platters of *pillo*
and pyramided high with a collection of the very finest
Persian food. Ali would take us to the kitchen, which
was a separate room not connected with the house, and
allow us to watch the cooks preparing the food on
the floor. They cooked over open brasiers, burning
charcoal or wood, depending on the particular food
being prepared. One cook was completely enshrouded
in a *chador* and veil.

"See that one in the veil? In all the years she has
been in the family, which is—Allah knows how many
—ever since she was born—none of the men has ever
seen her face. Did you notice how she always turns
her back to me when I enter?" Ali smiled.

"Aren't you curious to see what she looks like?"
Marlene asked.

"Not particularly. She probably looks much better
this way." Ali gestured toward her.

The four of us women were given one very large
room. Bedding was spread on the floor by servants
and the mattress pads covered with crisp colored sheets
brought from the States by the colonel's wife. These
were topped by elegant satin and velvet comforters.
My pale green velvet comforter was hand embroidered,
with an enormous peacock covering the entire surface.
It was quite an effort to crawl out of that comfortable bed in the mornings. When we first awakened
we had to rouse ourselves only enough to turn over to
sip the morning tea, all but poured into us by a servant.

The men had another large room with the same dormitory arrangement. At the Iranian New Year, *No-Ruz*,

around forty people are guests for many days in this home. One large room was devoted entirely to the storage of bedding. All upper-class Persian homes are equipped to accommodate as many relatives and friends as may wish to drop in at any time.

We visited the beautiful gardens for which this city is well known. Two of Persia's most illustrious poets, Saadi and Hafiz, are buried here in much revered tombs, surrounded by beautifully manicured gardens. We of the Western world are better acquainted with the works of Omar Khayyám, but he, to the Persians, is a lesser poet. He was a well-known mathematician and astronomer who composed quatrains from time to time to please his intimate friends. The verses enjoyed a certain popularity, but were later largely forgotten when the giants of Persian poetry greatly overshadowed him. He was almost forgotten in Iran for centuries until Edward FitzGerald translated his works. It is very difficult to translate from Persian and retain the full meaning and feeling.

The Persian values a poem for its beauty and for its usefulness in meeting the daily problems of life. If you would influence an Iranian, hire a poet. Politicians have long known they must employ poets to influence public opinion. The Anglo-Iranian oil controversies of the 1930's and the 1950's were discussed in poetry, as have been the Anglo-Russian agreement of 1907, the reforms of Reza Shah, the Allied invasion of Iran, and the attempt on the life of the present Shah. Verse is used to comment on public affairs as political cartoons are in the West.

Men who can recite the poets hour after hour from memory (even if they are illiterate) are respected and admired by everybody.

Our friends, and even our servants, quoted poetry fitting to the occasion or problem at the slightest provocation. Hafiz's book, *Divan*, is used alternately with the Koran to give an opinion when a decision has to be made.

Down the main boulevard we strolled and browsed in the shops, admiring the exquisite boxes made of camel bone, the finest in Persia. There was no hustle or bustle. The city seemed quiet and peaceful.

"Now I am going to show you a place which will make you think you have a trip home. Exactly as you have in the States," Ali said.

It was the new modern Nemazee Hospital, one of the best in the world. The staff of doctors includes outstanding American specialists as well as Iranian, and the institution itself boasts the most modern equipment obtainable. The inside shone with cleanliness and light.

Marlene and the Morgan children had waited patiently to see the bazaar. They had seen many bazaars in other towns but hoped here to get a glimpse of the tribespeople. The Kashghai tribesmen were in their encampments in Fars (province of which Shiraz is the capital). We didn't dare to venture into their sector, but hoped to glimpse them in the bazaar.

We were well rewarded. The bazaar was filled with milling tribespeople as well as villagers. Few foreigners ever go here, so we were a novelty. Crowds followed us and gathered at our every hesitation. We stopped to watch Sherm try to squeeze into a Kashghai coat. Even the largest was too small, but he was determined. He is a large man and they are small and wiry. Even the felt native hat would need to be stretched. He persevered until he had collected the entire outfit, sash, pants, and all.

When we turned to leave, we found ourselves hemmed in by a crowd of not much less than a hundred tribespeople, giggling, pointing, laughing, and gaping. They began touching us and feeling our clothing. We weren't sure whether they were friend or foe. Evidently word had been sent via the grapevine of our predicament because two gendarmes appeared and tried to disperse the crowd. The throng was most reluctant to leave.

We were equally intrigued with them, and I couldn't get enough of their gay, colorful costumes. I had always heard of the many petticoats worn by the women. They add them as the wealth of the husband increases and I was trying hard to decide who were the wealthiest. They keep adding a new one on top, then discard the oldest when it finally falls to pieces. Hundreds of yards of material go into them and the outer skirt. Of course, blue jeans would be the practical solution for the life they lead of migration and manual labor in the fields and mountains. I suggested this to Ali.

"They would never go for that. Their skirts are their pride and their passion," he said.

"Their faces are certainly weather - beaten, aren't they?" Alice observed.

"Naturally. Yours would be too if you lived in the

A Purchase at the Bazaar

sun, the wind, and the rain all of your life with little protection," Bill commented.

The Kashghais are primarily a Turkic-speaking group, though a few Arab- and even some Persian-speaking bands have allied themselves with them. It is reported they have about thirty thousand in Fars. Their annual migration from winter to summer pasturage is the longest in Iran. They resisted Reza Shah when he tried to disarm them, which led to the imprisonment and death of their chief. Other leaders have been banished and now live in California.

Additional important tribes are the Kurds (of which about a million live in Iran), Bakhtiari (the tribe of ex-Queen Soraya's father), Turkomen, Lurs, Baluchi, and lesser tribes of Arabs, Shahsevans, and Khamseh.

These nomads are the most picturesque element of the Iranian population, representing the best in physical type and bravery. Several ruling dynasties have come from tribal warriors. They have always furnished the backbone of the armies. They are a law unto themselves and are ruled by the strict authority of their elected or hereditary leaders, the khans. Many of the khans have excellent educations which they obtained in Europe. Some are sending their sons abroad to school. They usually own houses in towns or on the tribal lands, but they spend much of their time in the tents of their tribal groups.

Family life goes on in the black tents which are made of a tough goat's-hair cloth woven by the women. Floor coverings are usually rugs woven by the women or, in case they are of lesser means, thick felt mats;

the blankets are piled against one wall and along the other wall are copper utensils, goatskin containers for liquids, earthenware jars, and bags of grain.

Their flocks sustain their life. They furnish milk, butter, and cheese, and their wool is used for weaving and to sell in town. The fascinating jewelry worn by the women usually includes strings of old silver and gold coins and represents, along with their skirts (depending upon the tribe), the entire accumulated wealth of the family. Horses and guns are the other valuable property.

The men do the hunting and care for the flocks and the herds of horses. The women gather fuel, carry water, do the cooking, sewing, and weaving.

"I'm glad I got you out of there with all your clothes on. Wow! I'm ready for some tea or—I know, you must have the most famous food in Shiraz, *poluday*. It's kind of a sherbet made with snow and starch from rice. By the way, do you know the word sherbet (*sharbat*) is Persian? You lifted it right out of Farsi and put it into the English language," Ali declared.

"We did?" Marlene perked up. "Well, let's go get some. I'm starved."

Trailing behind, with Ali in the lead, we marched down the street and followed him into one of the tiny shops selling ice creams and sherbets.

"You do the ordering," Sherm said to him.

"Personally, I like the sherbet made from pomegranate juice, lemons, and oranges. Sometimes we add violets, oranges, and vinegar together, too. That's a popular one. Try them all! *Poluday* is the most famous, and this is the only city where they make it so good, so have that first."

As we ate the *poluday*, Sherm maintained, "I have never tasted anything quite like it. Delicious. And very refreshing."

The other sherbets came in for a sampling. "Gee, I could spend the day here. It's all so yummy. S'pose they need a professional taster?" Marlene inquired.

We peeked into several teahouses and cafes as we wandered on down the street. They are popular gathering places in all the towns, especially the villages. Here men drop in for friendly conversation, a game of backgammon (one of the most popular games among all classes), and to smoke their water pipes.

Tea is Persia's favorite drink and is served in glasses set in solid silver holders in wealthy homes, and in plain glasses to the man on the street, always with plenty of sugar. Often the drinker holds a lump of sugar between his teeth and sips the tea through it. The custom of tea drinking seems to have come from Russia in fairly recent times, for during the seventeenth and eighteenth centuries the Persians drank a great deal of coffee, which was quite unknown in the West until European travelers discovered it in Turkey and Iran.

"Look, there is some of the famous Shiraz tile with all the birds and flowers," I said as I spotted some in a plumbing shop. "Same as we saw at the poets' tombs."

I said to Ali, "You know, I thought tile was invented in Spain. Imagine my surprise to find out here is where it was perfected—then the conquerors took it to Spain, and ultimately it got to us. Another thing

I thought originated in Spain was castanets; now I learn they were using them in Persian court dances long before Spain got them. And charcoal—to think, you have been cooking over it for hundreds of years, not just for fun but out of necessity. Every time we have a barbecue in our patio, visions of the shish kebab street hawkers hovering over their charcoal stoves, fanning the flames, will appear before me."

The following day we were to see Persepolis, or Takht-i-Jamshid, as it is known to the Persians. We rented a good-sized car to take this trip over the rough and dusty roads to that historic site.

There are countries, such as Egypt, whose recorded history dates farther back than that of Iran. China's and Japan's existence as nations was never interrupted, whereas Iran suffered all the vicissitudes to which a nation may be exposed. However, none but Italy can pretend to have been so deeply interlaced with the fate of humanity as Iran. Her people never ceased to be important participants of the world drama, whatever the role.

Persepolis is a monument to the Achaemenid period (550-331 B.C.), two hundred years when Persia was at the height of power. The Medes had established an empire in the sixth century B.C. and ruled it briefly. Persians were one of the tribes which made up this empire.

With Cyrus the Great leading them, the Persians overthrew the Median Empire. Since he was of the Achaemenid clan, his dynasty was called by that name. He extended his domain to master the lands from the

Mediterranean to the Punjab and from the Nile to Turkistan. In one generation, a relatively obscure people had risen to rule these lands. This first glorious episode brings Iranian sighs for the past, and they constantly refer to their historical greatness.

This kingdom was the first great empire and exceeded that of the Roman Empire in extent. The language now became Persian, and the country became known as Persia, lasting for two hundred years.

After Cyrus came a weak leader, then Darius, who built a magnificent palace near the capital of Persepolis.

Long before we reached these ancient ruins, the tall pillars set against the cloudless blue sky first looked like matchsticks; then, as we came closer, their magnitude overwhelmed us.

Recently an enterprising soul has built a lovely motel at the foot of the Mount of Mercy, close to the excavations of the ancient palaces. Until then there was no place to stay. We quickly got settled and took off to explore.

If for no other reason, I shall never forget Persepolis because it is the first historic spot I have ever visited where there were no guides, no vendors, not even any other sight-seers—nobody to bother us. We enjoyed discovering it all by ourselves from our guidebook. Such a contrast to Babylon, the Egyptian pyramids, Baalbek, and other sight-seeing paradises where you are constantly being heckled by self-made guides.

At Persepolis was the ceremonial palace where the sovereigns spent the latter part of the winter and the early months of the spring. A discovery of clay tablets in the Treasury and Royal Accounts Office here makes it evident that no slave labor was used in erecting these edifices; instead, the kings gave large sums from their own treasury as daily wages. This was really progressive for the times.

The matchsticks seen from a distance turned out to be the great columns, doorways, and recesses of the immense halls reserved for the king and crown prince. They were constructed of stones of tremendous size, which were hewn from rock and cut with perfect accuracy.

The portraits of the king, his soldiers, and horses have a lifelike expression which is found on no other Asiatic work of art.

"Mother, look—can you believe it—you can see the singe marks where Alexander the Great burned and destroyed the palaces. I can't believe I am actually seeing the smoked walls that have stood like this all these centuries. Wait till I tell my history teacher back at Glendale. Isn't it exciting?" Marlene was wide-eyed.

I looked up at the monstrous pillar and, sure enough, there it was, just as Alexander had left it. No wonder, when you see the ruins of what was the world's most beautiful palace at this time, that he is so bitterly hated by the Persians. He destroyed all but the last vestiges of this once great nation.

SMALL WORLD

THE RAH-E NOV (THE NEW WAY) IRANIAN WOM-
en's Association flattered four of us American women
by inviting us to attend one of their meetings. In
April of 1955, nine courageous, well-educated women,
banded together and formed this group. It now has
a membership of eight hundred. Their purpose is to
awaken the women of Iran, so membership is not exclusive. If you are fifteen years of age or over, willing to work, and two women who are already members will sponsor you, you are as good as in. Their first
concern is to alleviate the conditions of the women's
prisons and to agitate for reforms in the existing marriage laws.

Every day some of the group meet to work on these
problems. They go to the prisons and teach reading,
writing, sewing, and other skills which can help to re-
habilitate the prisoners. They also want equality in
the inheritance laws. The existing law allows a man
to inherit just twice as much as a woman in the same
family. Furthermore, they would like to abolish polygamy. The fanatic mullahs are fighting them every inch
of the way. Even though they hold up Turkey as an
example of a good Moslem country which, thanks to
Ataturk, has abolished polygamy—this argument, as

yet, has had no effect on the religious leaders of Iran. I had watched with intense interest any signs of women's fight for freedom.

The present system of laws had its origin in the old religious law as expounded by Mohammed in the Koran. He did not claim to be the founder of a new religion, as his mission was to restore the earlier religions to their pristine purity. Islam (meaning absolute submission to the will of God) is the correct name of the faith, and the followers are called Muslims (Moslems). It is a man's religion and Iran is still a man's world. Mohammed made this clear in the Koran. It says, "Men are in charge of women, because Allah hath made the one of them to excel the other." In another section he said, "Women are fields to be plowed." This would make any woman indignant until she goes deeper into his teachings and realizes the conditions of his times.

Actually, Mohammed was one of the greatest champions of women's rights the world has ever known. Because of him, the horrible practice of female infanticide, prevalent among the pagan Arabs, was abrogated. He condemned the inheriting of the widow with the rest of an estate as though she were chattel. Because of him, women were allowed to inherit a share of the property of their husbands and kinsfolk. Although only half as much as a man, it was better than what they had been getting before—nothing.

Polygamy was widely practiced at this time and was lawful. Along with unrestricted concubinage there was a most disastrous effect on the entire social and moral structure, which Mohammed did much to remedy. He never ceased to champion the cause of women against the ill treatment of his contemporaries.

The prophet married Khadija, who was fifteen years his senior, and took no other wife during the twenty-six years of their married life. Not until after her death did he become a polygamist when he took other wives, mostly old maids and widows left destitute and without protection.

We Christians certainly do not take the Bible as seriously as the Koran is taken. If we did, we women would really have a battle on our hands. In the New Testament, mostly from Paul, the following admonitions are given, "Wives, submit yourselves unto your husbands, as unto the Lord. For the husband is the head of the wife, even as Christ is the head of the church. . . . Neither was the man created for the woman; but the woman for the man . . . I would have you know that . . . the head of the woman is the man. . . . Likewise, ye wives, be in subjection to your own husbands."

The present women's struggle in Iran is for a broader interpretation of Mohammed's teachings to suit the age.

Men, as a rule, not the women, get the divorce, and it's easy. In the Shi'a sect, which is the leading one of Iran, a man need give no reason but only has to say "I divorce you," three times before a magistrate, and it is done. Women take back their maiden names. Since *knome* (lady) goes for both Miss and Mrs., this does not create a problem.

The only possible way a woman can secure a divorce from her husband in Iran is to *prove* he is insane and her life is in danger, or that he fails to provide.

A man can legally have four wives, and as many concubines as he wishes. From economic pressures and some imitation of Western culture, polygamy is rapidly vanishing in the upper classes. In the villages and among the tribes and lower classes it is still practiced. Men need the wives to assist with the work in the fields and with the cattle.

The concubine or "contract wife" is a temporary wife to be kept in a separate establishment for a stated period of days, weeks, or months. The contract states her reward. However, in the event of the father's death, what children she may have are completely dependent on the mercies of the first wife's children for inheritance. Women reformists are concerned with what happens to the children after the concubine is divorced, as well as with polygamy producing too many children for one father to feed.

We personally knew only two instances where a man had more than one wife. Our closest neighbor had two wives. As told to us by our servants, the first wife could not bear children, so she selected the second wife. The second one evidently came through, because there were three vociferous youngsters in the next compound.

Marriage is on a different basis than in our country. Companionship of the man and woman are not the primary concern. A wife's role is to bear children. If she is wealthy, she oversees the caring of the children, and everything that goes into running a household. If poor, she will do all this herself, and maybe work besides as a servant. This seems backward to those few of us women in the world who have newly gained freedom, but it wasn't too long ago in most of the world that women were believed not even to have souls.

When I narrated to my Persian lady friends of the upper classes what would be expected of them if they gained the same freedom as that of an American wife, they weren't quite sure if it was worth it. They wanted what we have with our legal rights, plus their servants, but not all of our obligations. When I told them, "Only 10 per cent of our women have ever had any kind of help in their homes," they were aghast. "We have no servant class, and a wife is expected to be a mother, sweetheart, nurse, hair dresser, seamstress, cook, chauffeur, accountant"—I didn't dare name the other expectations—"then with the time left over, if there is any, we are expected to contribute to the less fortunate and to our community."

To some harrassed, overworked American wives and mothers, the life of a wealthy Iranian woman might be enviable. She is queen in her own home. Her husband has no part in running the household, and she has complete command of the servants. Her function is to be and remain a beautiful doll for him to come home to, and to bear his children. She spends her days at the beauty parlor, in the bath houses being massaged and scrubbed, at the dressmakers, shoemakers, gossiping, or playing cards with her women friends.

Although there are fourteen newly organized women's clubs around Tehran, as a rule the Iranian woman is not fired with any philanthropic fervor. For the most part she would rather go along with the beliefs of the older generation such as, "Allah gives money to those who can handle it."

At the "New Way" meeting I had the good fortune to be placed next to a most attractive Persian woman who spoke English and translated the speeches for me. She told me that her daughter was attending college in Los Angeles, and that she had just spent a year there herself, returning only four months ago. Hardly looked old enough to be out of college herself. She must have caught this expression from me as she went on to explain that she was married at sixteen to a man selected by her family.

"My daughter lives with some wonderful friends, Mr. and Mrs. Bernard Scott."

"You don't mean Ruth Scott, by any chance," I squealed.

She almost jumped out of her California coat. "How did you know?" she asked.

"You must be Mrs. Niami."

"Yes, yes, I am."

"Ruth Scott is a very good friend of mine. She told me all about you and your daughter and asked me to look you up. We have wandered up and down Naderi many times trying to find your husband's place of business. It's the only address we have for you."

She laughed. "Of course, you couldn't find it because his sign is in Persian."

Immediately we felt like old friends and began whispering about personal things until we realized we were distracting the speaker.

As the meeting progressed, my admiration for these women kept increasing. I was very impressed with the intelligent speeches and reports on the strides which had been made in women's prison reform. First they would speak in Persian, then again in English for the Americans. It was interesting to learn they had enlisted the help of many outstanding men in their push for women's rights.

After the meeting I asked so many questions that the hostess invited Mrs. Niami and me to stay on. We had an enlightening discourse about the differences between Western and Eastern culture.

"One thing I would especially like to learn about, firsthand, is your marriage customs. I have been invited to a Moslem wedding in a few days and it would be helpful to know more about these things," I said.

Mrs. Ashraf, the hostess, started off by explaining, "Our first families have great pride. It is very important to a man's career and future to marry into the right family. It works both ways, and the girl's family stands to profit by the proper liaison as well. Marriages are arranged by the families, and it is considered desirable for cousins to marry, especially on the father's side."

Mrs. Niami added, "You see in Iran you get acquainted with your husband *after* marriage instead of before. We assume and hope that love, affection, and respect will come as we live together."

"I know that has been and is the accepted way of

mating in the Orient and Middle East, and even to a lesser degree in some parts of Europe. From the *Tehran Journal* (English-language newspaper published by Iranians) I have noticed that the statistics for your divorce rate are slightly higher than those of the States, so your system must work or fail, whichever you want to call it, just about as well as ours," I said.

"Occasionally, love becomes very deep between a husband and wife here. Of course, we have lots of the other kind of marriages, too, where the partners are not well suited, and then we have the same problems they have anywhere else in the world," Mrs. Niami added. "The double standard is the only one accepted here. A man can do almost anything as far as his relations with women are concerned, without criticism. But a woman has to guard her life very carefully so that it will not reflect in any way upon her husband or her children."

Mrs. Ashraf reflected, "The first time a girl has any freedom is when she is married. Up until this time there is so much at stake for her and her family that she is carefully guarded. If there is evidence that the bride is not a virgin, her husband can send her home, and that terminates the marriage at once."

"I have seen so many items in the *Tehran Journal*, which bear out just what you have said," I commented. "That column of 'Events and Accidents' has intrigued me so much. Noticed just last week the title has been changed to 'Comedies and Tragedies of Human Life Retold,' which is most descriptive of the contents."

An example from the *Tehran Journal* which pertains to the above conversation is quoted below.

TEHRAN — Shortly after entering bridal chamber hysterical groom causes immense commotion, claiming bride is not virgin. Medical examination belies claim but unreasonable groom is not satisfied. Next morning case is taken to court and court's doctor affirms bride's virginity. Satisfied, groom proceeds to take bride home but later refuses, saying this is a bad start for any life.

If a girl is unfortunate enough to become pregnant before marriage it is considered in some families the honorable duty of her brother or father, no matter how beloved she is, to kill her. He may get a few years in prison, but he and his family feel he must sacrifice himself to avenge the family honor. There were many reports on these cases. One is quoted below from the same column:

BANDAR ABBAS — Learning about his sister's improper conduct, married man takes her for picnic outside town and tries to throw her off a cliff. Just as she is being pushed off the cliff she clings to her brother and takes him with her. They both die in hospital.

Frequently, the girl commits suicide. The papers were full of these tragedies. Another way the family disposes of this problem is to throw the girl out of the family, deny her existence, and disown her. In the upper-class families among the less fanatical they will often try to hire someone to marry her.

Another excerpt shows the violent feeling of the family against violating a girl.

KASHAN — Infuriated mob attacks home of man who raped teen-age girl and then fled village. Mobsters give same treatment to escaped man's mother and sister and then, to top it all, cut off ears of his young brother.

The following indicates the humble position of women:

TEHRAN — A 45 year old husband is asked to get a divorce by his 18 year old wife but says "Divorce? Over my dead body." So far so good, because this goes to show how fond he is of preventing matrimonial edifice from collapsing. But the question the court has to decide is this: Does a man who refuses to support his wife, who has two other wives and who constantly beats his wife, have the right to refuse a divorce?

This item is amusing for the reader, although I am sure the wife wouldn't be able to say the same.

RASHT — Expressing wish over bottle of vodka to have good time, married man is advised by helpful friend that for modest consideration he can take him to exclusive house where they will be entertained by woman operating incognito. Everything goes on like clockwork until woman makes her entrance, to be greeted by her husband's petrified gaze. The scene that followed is being left to the readers' imagination.

"Is it ever possible for a boy and girl to select their own mates?" I asked.

"Frankly, to tell you the truth, Iran is in transition, and tradition is becoming confused. At the present time I would say there are about three ways of making a marriage. The traditional one is still the most prevalent—the families make all the arrangements without consulting the two parties most concerned. They do not meet until the legal ceremony," said Mrs. Ashraf.

"The young men educated abroad are demanding a peek, at least, at their future brides. You know the new German department store, Forushgahe Ferdowsi, is becoming quite a rendezvous for this sort of thing. By prearrangement the boy manages to walk by with friends just as the girl passes with her relatives—then they take a quick glance. Other ways are when friends make arrangements to get the two together in the same social group where they may get a glimpse of one another. Sometimes they may even direct a few remarks to each other in the presence of the group, but usually they feign indifference. Once in a while, walking to and from school, the boy and girl may begin to steal quick looks. This is not considered proper, however. If some of these things go on long enough, the pair may imagine themselves to be in love and plead with the parents of the boy to call upon the parents of the girl. If a marriage is so arranged, however, it is guarded from the public, and all carry on as if it had emanated directly from the parents." Mrs. Niami was candid.

"I have heard it rumored that some youngsters are going so far as to meet in a dark *kutche* at night and even hold hands. Among my acquaintances, I don't know how this could be accomplished as the girls are watched incessantly," I observed.

"It wouldn't happen to my daughter if she were here." Mrs. Niami became excited. "What gossip if it were ever discovered! Maybe this will help you to understand why mothers as well as fathers are so proud to have boys. There is so much liability in having girls."

"Daughters are entirely subject to the father's authority and only the father and grandfather (if the father is dead) have the legal right to impose marriage under the age of puberty. Mothers or female family members may initiate the arrangements for the marriage of their son, but the final settlement is between the family heads. For all intents and purposes, the husband is the boss, but in many cases the Iranian woman has greater influence on his decisions and attitudes than a Western wife has on her husband."

Mrs. Niami went on. "This is one place where mothers have strong influence over their sons. When a mother decides it is time for her boy to marry, she starts shopping for a girl just about like you would shop in the bazaar. When it comes to making final arrangements, the negotiations between the families are also similar —much bargaining."

"I have heard of some of the Iranian men going to tea at their betrothed's home before they are married. Is this proper?" I asked.

"In very modern families — everything here at the present depends on the particular family — the son sometimes does go along with his mother when a suitable girl has been found, and they steal some rather indirect looks."

"Now, what if the girl isn't satisfied after seeing the boy?" I innocently asked.

"It is up to the girl to satisfy, not be satisfied," Mrs. Ashraf broke in. "Usually the girls are not consulted. A man is a man in our country and they feel that is all that is necessary. Sometimes a girl is allowed to express herself, but it depends on the family whether it carries any weight or not."

"After they go through all this and everything is arranged, then I understand it is up to the man's family to foot the bill for the wedding," I stated.

"That's right. Oh, this is a big event, and even poorer-class families have to stage a big party and a feast for their neighbors and friends. In the upper-class families the cost would start somewhere around five thousand dollars and go all the way up to a fortune. In many cases the family goes into debt deep enough to remain debtors the rest of their lives," Mrs. Ashraf commented.

"Are things done this same way in the villages and tribes?" I inquired.

"With some variations. Each tribe and village has a little different tradition. In the tribes the women have never been veiled and the boys and girls work together, so have an opportunity to, at least, see one another before marriage, although it is still arranged by the families. This is also true in the villages."

"What is the legal age of marriage here?" I quizzed.

"Sixteen, but nine is the accepted age in Islam. It is possible to persuade some mullahs to perform the ceremony according to religious law. However, this is a crime both for the mullah and the husband, but it is kept secret and not registered until the legal age. A great percentage of the marriages are contracted under age.

"In the villages they usually marry younger than sixteen. A girl is considered an old maid when she gets beyond about twelve. My servant's nine-year-old daughter has a best friend who is a married matron of ten and her husband is nineteen. The married one and my servant's little girl play dolls and house all day long, then the married one goes to her own home and keeps house for real." Mrs. Niami smiled incredulously.

From the *Tehran Journal* there were many instances of these child marriages—one:

ABADAN — Eight year old girl "married" to 45 year old man is promised by cradle-snatcher she will not be accosted for the next seven years, but word is broken as soon as couple leave hometown, Borudird. Now, girl, frightened and shelterless, has taken refuge in police station, weepingly asking to be sent to her parents.

I really enjoyed this tidbit. Thought it served the old fossil right:

YAZD — Seventy-five year old man asks for hand of 15 year old girl but is cheated into marrying her 49 year old mother, a widow with nine children. As marriage is legal in every respect, man is finding himself saddled with a wife of 49 instead of 15.

"In spite of these very young marriages, we are really progresssive compared to our neighbors, Afghanistan, Arabia, and Yemen. There the women are still veiled. When Reza Shah took over, he made it illegal even to drive a woman anyplace who was wearing a veil. The police would snatch the veils from the women in the streets. For the older generation this was hard because to them it was as if they were left standing naked in public. Since Reza Shah, the women have gone back to the *chador* as you can see. We lost a little ground on that. Our group is fighting for many things. We still don't have the vote and no right to hold office, which keeps us a limited, inferior race apart. This will take time and effort just as it did in your country," Mrs. Ashraf added.

A few evenings later, my new-found friend, Mrs. Niami, and her husband came to our home to attend an open house we were giving.

Mr. Niami had lived for fourteen years in the States and had amusing control of our slang and manners. He and Sherm kept eyeing one another. "It's the dog-gonedest thing, but you look familiar to me," Mr. Niami said.

"You know, I was thinking the same thing. Maybe we have passed on the street or been at the same restaurant, something like that," Sherm returned.

We all exchanged the usual polite conversation of a first meeting, introduced them around, then asked, "Where did you live in the States?"

"Lived in Minnesota first. Did my undergraduate work at Carleton College, then went on to North-western——" Sherm only let him get as far as "North-western."

"That's it—Carleton," Sherm yelled.

Suddenly they fell upon one another's necks in front of everyone and Mr. Niami was shouting, "Sherm Miller, you old reprobate, you haven't changed a bit," and Sherm was saying, "Abbey, the Sheik! You're still handsome, but you lost some of your hair and changed your name."

When they settled down enough to tell us the story we learned that they had spent four years in college together, graduating in the same class, and knew one another very well. Mr. Niami remembered Sherm as the big football star and athlete, and Sherm remembered him as the only Middle Easterner the school had ever seen and whom they called "the Sheik."

"I would have recognized your name 'Abbey' in a minute. Why did you change it?"

"When I left Persia nobody had a last name. We were just known by the son-of-so-and-so. While I lived in the States, Reza Shah made his *coup d'état*. He demanded that everyone have an identification card and choose a last name. When I went to the States I just took my father's given name as we all did and used it for a last name. The family chose Niami. Been quite recent that the people in this country have had last names."

"That must have been fun to be able to choose your own name," I said.

"Usually we took names that had something to do with our father's profession, or just because we liked the sound of it—like they did in Europe. Something like your name, 'Miller.' Probably some of your forebears were millers," said Mr. Niami.

"Must be rugged on the genealogy," Sherm remarked.

Mrs. Niami laughed good-naturedly. "You would be surprised how we can trace ourselves back to important rulers. It's harder for the women, though, as we are never included in the family tree."

"Why? Don't you resent that?" I put in.

"Nothing we can do about it. Suppose it would be very complicated if they did include the women because think of all those plural marriages, and the wives in one family would take up a whole book if the entire harem was included."

"My wife is of the Kajar dynasty, the one overthrown by Reza Shah. She is of royalty on both sides and still many people call her princess. That family tree is simple in that, for her, this only has to be traced to her grandfather. Lot of branches on all the royal family trees, though—so many children. We have had so many kings, too," Mr. Niami concluded.

Mr. Niami sent his driver home to bring back his Carleton annual. After the other guests had left, the men spent a nostalgic evening way back in Northfield, Minnesota, while Mrs. Niami and I were subjected to hearing about their many exploits and misty-eyed accounts of college life. What a small world.

I DO

Not realizing how difficult it is for a non-Moslem to attend a legal wedding ceremony, I had expressed myself to several people about how much I would like to see one.

We had come to know a very beautiful girl, Mina, who worked in the library at the university, and the man, Mostafa, she was going to marry, who was a close friend of Ali. We never saw the betrothed couple together, naturally, until they were married, but on the strength of that double friendship, we were invited to the legal ceremony. Secretly, we found out this had taken a lot of arranging as a special favor to us. Either the mullahs who perform the ceremony would not be able to see us, or, like a few very modern and tolerant ones, would allow it. I suspect that since the mullahs never saw us and we were told to quietly fade into the crowd, that it was hoped our presence would not be discovered by them.

The morning of the ceremony we were alerted by Mina to be on the route from her fiancé's home to hers, in order to watch the porters transport the traditional wedding gifts.

Trudging down the road they came, balancing huge

trays of gifts on their heads. The lead porter had an elegant large silver mirror and silver candlesticks along with a few other items on his tray. The others tramped behind him with their trays filled with incense, fruit, small chests (no doubt filled with jewelry), and many other interesting but, from our vantage point, undistinguishable presents.

I craned my neck in the hope of seeing piles of rare and unusual dress fabrics which must be included. The minimum required is five dress lengths and runs up to any amount which the groom can afford.

This is an especially profitable day for the porters, because the bride's family tips generously at this once in a lifetime occasion.

The legal ceremony is small and select (as contrasted to the reception) with only relatives and close friends in attendance. There were about fifty people at this one. The ceremony takes place in the bride's home, but the contract money given by the groom is used to pay for the wedding dress, ring, and accompanying expenses for this and the later wedding reception. In this case the reception took place one month afterward.

The women were all in one room, the men in another. The bride sat alone on a special tapestry rug in still another room. Two mullahs stood outside her door and read from the Koran while she scanned the holy book, reviewing the story about Mohammed conquering Mecca.

The room in which the bride is seated must be on the first floor of the house, if possible—without basement or anything underneath. This is symbolic of the wedding being on a solid foundation. The ceremony must take place in the afternoon, before sundown, usually around four o'clock, and lasts from one to two hours.

On one side of the bride was a specially prepared, long, wide flap of bread, surrounded by vegetables. Bread is the symbol of God's blessing. If a Persian comes upon a piece of bread in the street, he will never step on it, and may even kiss it and put it aside where it would not be desecrated.

At her other side was a beautiful rug made of colored seeds of incense scattered into an intricate pattern. The size of the incense rug depends upon the wealth of the family. In this case it was very large. Directly in front of her was the lovely silver mirror. In the old days, the first time a bride saw her husband was in a mirror when he walked into the room after the ceremony. On each side of this stood the silver candelabra with candles burning. A picture of Ali (the founder of the Shi'a sect) was also in front of her. On the right was a plate of honey and butter and one of small white candies mixed with gold coins. After the ceremony, these coins were rained over the heads of the newly mated couple, and friends scrambled for the cherished mementos.

Although the necessary minimum is two women, in this case there were four who entered. I had been told by Mina, ahead of time, that these women must be happy in their married life and either relatives or close friends of the family. One symbolically rubbed

Gifts for the Bride

sugar between her hands above a sheet. This is to make the bride sweet for her husband. With seven different colors of thread, another sewed on the sheet, which is to close the mouths of the new relatives.

Incense in a charcoal burner was then whirled around the bride's head. This was to keep the evil eye away and dispel any bad omens.

The mullahs then asked her if she accepted Mostafa for a husband. There was silence. She was asked again. No answer. Someone forgot to tell me she had to be asked three times so I began to worry for fear she had changed her mind. Then the third time she said, *"Balle."* Joyous shouts went up from the guests.

She then peered into the mirror and watched her husband enter the room. He went to the mother-in-law, kissed her hand, and asked permission to kiss the bride. He threw back Mina's veil, lifted her to her feet and kissed her gently. As is custom she did not return the kiss or show animation over it. The bride then placed her hand on his head to indicate that he would obey her. They then stepped through the religious chapters of the Koran which had been written on cloth and tied together to make a large circle.

Next, the bride took off one shoe and extinguished the candles. At this moment, someone plunked a small boy on her lap. Mina told me afterward this was in the hope that her first-born would be a boy.

She took some honey from the plate and put it in the groom's mouth. He returned the ritual in the same way (this was to sweeten them both).

The guests rushed to the bride, the father and brothers

kissed her, the men kissed one another on the cheeks, women kissed each other. No kissing of the bride and groom by the opposite sex like at our weddings—never! This is considered the road to adultery.

Lastly, the bride and groom are put in a room alone. Often this is the first time they have ever spoken to one another or even seen one another. In this case the couple had enjoyed tea a few times with the family in Mina's home, but had never been alone.

Sherm gave me a knowing smile, but he didn't know that shortly afterward they would emerge for the dinner and refreshments, then the groom goes to his home and the bride stays in hers.

Weeks later the couple showed us the registry which was brought to the bride to sign during the course of the ceremony. They had been given a miniature copy for themselves. They translated it. First it mentioned the exact dowry as given by the groom to the bride, which was a beautiful and expensive Koran, mirror, two candlesticks of silver and named their value, one diamond ring, its value; other items; then the cash amount already paid and the amount to be kept on hand. The bride can collect the full amount on demand or have the husband jailed if he doesn't pay. This is a device to prevent divorce. All of this is in writing.

Since a marriage can be for any length of time here, the kind of marriage has to be specified. In this case it said "permanent."

There is a place for conditions of marriage. The most common one nowadays is to specify that he cannot take another wife.

Now from this time until the wedding reception they cannot live together. It is a get-acquainted time, much like our engagement period. Usually, nowadays, it is a matter of months before they live together, depending on the decision of the families.

We cornered Ali and Sherm asked, "How long before they start living together?"

"I don't know," he answered. "They are going to have the reception in a month. Sometime after that. Two or three months is popular now, but usually it is a year. They have to find a place to live and get everything ready. I have friends who have been married for seven years and haven't lived together yet."

"Good heavens! What is holding them up?" My mouth fell open.

"They can't work out the arrangements to suit everyone, but they are legally married and neither can marry anyone else unless the husband divorces her."

"Is this common?" asked Sherm.

"No, this is an exception, but it really does go on for a few years in some instances. Then again, very modern couples, once in a while, will announce to everyone that this legal one is the final ceremony and they will start living together."

A month later we went to the reception in the swank University Club. It could have been anywhere in the States. There was a beautiful tiered wedding cake which was cut according to Western custom. There was no receiving line. The couple strolled about the hall, greeting and shaking hands with each guest as two little flower girls followed holding up the bride's train. There were several hundred guests, and tables with wonderful food.

Some girl in the crowd usually dances to the traditional wedding music. In this case it was a little girl. This dance is improvised. In retrospect, this reception was the simplest and nearest to our American traditional ones of any we saw during our two years in Iran, and we saw a number of them.

After this first experience we became chronic uninvited wedding reception guests—thanks to Ali.

We could hear Ali's horn blowing to announce his approach up our holey *kutche*. "What I really came for is to invite you to my cousin's wedding reception tomorrow." Ali thrust an invitation into Sherm's hand. It was a single velvet-smooth piece of paper done in gold, Persian printing. Ali translated. The wording was much more elaborate than ours would have been and no answer was expected.

"Nobody will know the difference anyway. There will be about two thousand guests," said Ali. "As long as you have the invitation to present at the gate, that's all you need."

This reception was held at the Air Force Officers' Club. Ali had briefed us on the story of this match. His male cousin was forty-two and the girl seventeen. The cousin had been sent by his employer to drive this niece, her mother, brother, and aunt to Tehran from a southern province. The girl decided she was desperately in love with the cousin and let him or his family have no peace until he consented to marry her. Through the relatives, she had conspired to have his mother go to her family, and before the man knew what happened to him, he was betrothed.

Ali found it all very amusing, due to the fact that the cousin had long since given up the idea of marriage, and also that his bald head would attract such a young and beautiful girl.

Many important people were present. The two most famous popular Persian orchestras and the outstanding one of Iran, which played our popular music, and the two leading singers of the country furnished the entertainment. The very progressive Iranians, along with us, danced. There was the contrast of older women in *chadors* and women wearing the latest of Paris fashions.

Varicolored neon lights were everywhere. The dance floor was set around the immense garden pool. Yards and yards of tables were heaped with food. This was a very gala affair.

By way of contrast Sherm was invited by Ali to a male servant's wedding reception in the very poorest section of South Tehran. He and Ali were welcomed by the cheering guests about a mile before they reached the humble home. The driver showed his great surprise and could hardly believe that Ali and his American friend *really* came. What a great honor! They were ushered to the best seats. Somehow, two silver tea glass holders were borrowed to serve tea to these very special guests. The courtyard was crowded with chairs and tables arranged so that they faced a small stage in the center. Every chair was taken, and they were squeezed in so tightly that the servants could barely pass with the tea and cookies.

Ali told Sherm that the groom has to put on this show and feast for all his friends and neighbors, whether he can afford it or not. It often continues for five or six days. In addition, he has to buy all the wife's clothes.

Here was a poor man who made, at the maximum, the equivalent of eight dollars a week, who has to spend two or three hundred dollars for this event, as much as he would make in a year. If he doesn't have the money he must borrow it, and if he borrows it at the bazaar, he must pay 25 to 30 per cent interest on the money.

Entertainment consisted of a three-piece orchestra, a clarinet, violin, and accordion. The guests were all men, and so were the singers and dancers, although some were women impersonators. Many of the songs were off color—strictly for male consumption.

After a few hours watching his own party from the seat of honor, facing the stage, the groom excused himself and set off to return with the bride.

The women and children were on the second floor, hanging out of the windows watching the show. When the groom returned with his bride, the couple went to the second floor where a room had been prepared for them.

There was much shouting and clapping of hands. Ali took Sherm up the stairway and they were able to see twelve or fifteen women dressed in *chadors* come from the room, leaving the couple with just one woman who remained to secure evidence that the new wife had never belonged to another man.

NIGHT LIFE

THE NIAMIS INVITED US TO A DINNER AND DANCING party at the Park Hotel in company with several of their Iranian friends, plus Ali, whom they had met and enjoyed at our home.

The setting could have been any hotel in the world. The atmosphere was cosmopolitan, the Italian band played all the newest popular tunes, the food was delicious and beautifully served, the Iranian women elegantly dressed.

As a rule, Iranians are excellent dancers and Mrs. Niami's compliment to Sherm after they had danced was, "You are a very good dancer. You dance like an Iranian, not an American."

"I'm surprised to see all these people dancing, just as we Westerners do," I remarked to Ali.

"A few years ago this would have been unthinkable," he replied. "Men and women never danced together. This is all Western influence and everyone here tonight is very Westernized. There are only married couples here with the exception of perhaps a handful of women who are divorced or widowed or of bad reputation. These would not be virtuous women. The Niamis exchanged dances with you. This is inconceivable for a devout Moslem. I would never allow another man to dance with my wife."

"You mean if you marry, you won't let your wife dance with my husband? He is perfectly safe." I laughed.

"My wife will dance with no one but me, but if I ever do allow her to dance with another man it would be your husband. He is good."

The rounds had been made and Ali and I were left alone at the table. Sherm danced by. "Come on, why don't you two dance."

"Good idea," I said, and looked at Ali.

He flushed and stared straight ahead.

"Would it be because you are a devout Moslem, or because you are not Western enough to dance with me?" I asked.

"Yes, and because you are a married woman. You will find out how we feel about these things after you have been here longer."

"Oh, I'm sorry."

He looked furtively around the room, stood up, and bravely said, "Come on, we will dance."

With trepidation I made it to the floor, wondering every step if he knew how to dance. I could have saved my worry. He glided away like an old pro and Arthur Murray could have learned a few steps from him. He kept me at arm's length, looked neither right nor left, and tried to get lost in the crowd.

His duty performed, he bowed me to my place and I noted an expression of relief and a low sigh as he sank into his chair.

"You know, I am a judge. Well, it is actually written in the law that a judge is not to be frivolous. We are not to consume liquor or to dance."

"Oh, dear, what will they do with you now? Take your judgeship away?" I questioned in alarm.

"Hope not." He smiled reassuringly.

The longer I lived in Iran the more I appreciated the awkward predicaments into which we were always, very innocently, putting poor Ali.

"Does this law apply only to public frivolity?" I asked.

His eyes danced naughtily. "Only public. Ah, who knows what one does in private?"

Although Ali claimed not to be a very strong Moslem I would say he is one of the finest Moslems, Christians, Buddhists, or what have you that I have ever known. He has that basic sympathetic feeling for humanity along with the ingrained virtues and morals for which all religions strive.

Another popular night spot, especially in summer, is one of His Majesty's hotels, the Darband. This is located at the foot of the mountains in Tajrish, a stone's throw from us in Shimran. It is considered the ultimate for dinner dancing and luncheons. When I wanted to see the fashion forecast for the coming season I went there. There is no lovelier place anywhere than the Darband gardens on a summer evening. These are the kind of nights which must have inspired "The Thousand and One Nights." No wonder the poets of Persia were destined to write of these evenings of Oriental mystery.

All night life proved to be comparable with what we have in the States. There are many small night clubs and cabarets. The most famous truly Iranian club, frequented mostly by Iranians and until of late unknown to foreigners, is the Chekofe (Blossom Club). Ali took us there.

A beautiful Iranian girl sat directly facing Ali at the next table. All evening he had watched her out of the corner of his eye as he fingered his *tizbah* and looked self-conscious. She was with her family. Before the evening was over he was determined to learn her name.

"That girl over there reminds me just a little of my old girl back in the States," he reminisced.

"Tell us about the one in the States. Was it serious —the way you felt about her?" I asked.

A wistful expression came over his face. "Marvelous girl. Taught me English and how to dance. I met her when I was just learning English. Didn't even know enough of it to carry on a conversation. This was way back when we were both students at Queens College in New York."

"How did you converse, if you didn't speak English?" I quizzed.

He fastened me with his piercing eyes. "In the universal language—the language of love." He hesitated, slightly embarrassed.

"Oh," I exclaimed, "but you were a good Moslem boy. What would you know about such things?"

"When I left Iran, I was twenty-two and a very innocent boy. I hadn't even as much as held the hand

of a girl. There is no opportunity for that, and besides it is morally incorrect for a good Moslem to touch
a woman until her hand is placed in his at the marriage
ceremony. My indoctrination was sudden and overwhelming. Wow!" Ali chuckled.

"It's a long story how it happened. My boat reservations got mixed up and I arrived in Italy without
any way to get to America. I went to the Iranian
consulate and after a lot of red tape, I was put aboard
an army transport along with three other Iranian boys,
and ten Arabs, fourteen of us men in all. This boat
was different," he chortled. "It was a boat full of six
hundred war brides going to their husbands in the States.
Oh, boy, what a trip! They were wild. Hadn't seen
their husbands or many men for a long time. I finally
had to lock my door and hide under the bed as they
pounded and shouted for me to come out. It was a
very lively crossing and, believe me, an educational one."
He shook his head wearily. "Oh, boy! Oh, boy!"

"Then you were well prepared for life in the States?"
Sherm declared.

"Well—I'd say somewhat, but even to this day I'm
not prepared to look at women and men kissing one
another at train stations and airports, anyplace in public. Just can't stand it."

I wanted to hear more about the American girl so
I leaned over the table and said, "Tell us more about
the girl from Queens College."

"You want to know if I liked her very much—
O.K., the answer is yes. There are quite a number of
American girls married to Iranians living here, but

often it is difficult for everyone involved. It is the custom for the sons and wives to live with the son's family for the first few years of marriage. An Iranian girl is brought up to accept this. American girls are too independent to have the decisions made by the mother-in-law and older members of the man's family. Also, it is difficult to learn the language without a heavy accent, and her days would have to be spent with other women. Another thing, the wife is expected to take the husband's religion. So many complications." He slapped his head.

"Persians are so adaptable. You could have lived with her in the States like many Persians have done with their American wives, and the problems would have been minimized," I offered.

"I am an Iranian. I am proud of it. Iran is my home, and I would never be truly happy living elsewhere."

"Was that your first—well—er—serious affair?" I asked.

"I was betrothed to my cousin before I left Iran. I had seen her a few times. When I returned, our family had a gathering and she was there. She danced with others of my cousins and friends. I decided she was neither Iranian nor Western—nothing. I left the party, and the engagement was broken."

"Didn't that cause family friction?" Sherm interjected.

"It certainly did, but I just couldn't accept her for a wife after that. A well-bred Iranian girl does not dance with lots of men."

All the time we lived in Iran Ali's mother was anxious to find just the right bride for him and so were his cousins and friends. He said it had gone on for years like that. Every other day it was a new girl, but Ali kept his counsel and let the women of the family entertain themselves by calling on prospective families, while he casually vetoed them all.

The high light of the late fall social season was Queen Soraya's ball. We were lucky to be able to attend the last ball shortly before she was divorced by the Shah.

It was an important affair, first, to celebrate the liberation of the northern province of Azerbaijan from Russia, and secondly, for charity. During the second World War, Russia moved into the north, the British took the south, and the Americans were also in Iran. All the Allies promised to get out when it was all over. The Russians refused to leave and clung tenaciously to this province for a few years until the United Nations brought enough pressure and sentiment to bear to get them out.

In company with another American couple, Loreine and Tom Foley, we rode in style in a chauffeur-driven limousine to the famous Iranian Officers' Club. This club was built by Reza Shah to be the most luxurious of its kind in the world. I haven't seen all the others, but this is magnificent.

Our car entered the courtyard and was driven around the circular driveway. The entire building was outlined in colored lights, and looked like a movie set. The paths were lined with the Shah's personal guard.

Footmen and doormen fell all over themselves to assist us as we swept in.

We were ushered up a wide, graceful, center staircase over which hung a crystal chandelier of great proportions. Exquisite Persian carpets covered every foot of the building.

When we looked around, we realized why separate invitations had to be issued—one for men and one for women. It was obvious that most people had not been accompanied by one of the opposite sex. One entire wall was crowded with young, evidently eligible, girls and about half as many men lined the opposite wall. It was a long way across that ballroom to throw insinuating glances, but I am told there is always the hope for a girl that she will inspire some man's family who is shopping for a bride to take more than a passing glance. Except for this, it could have been a charity ball anywhere.

Without fanfare, Queen Soraya quietly entered the ballroom and made her way across it after a few of us were gently removed from her path.

All at once we found ourselves practically alone in the ballroom. Lines of people were rushing madly as to a fire. We joined the exodus and found it led to the buffet tables downstairs.

The feast was spread out on many long tables and included stuffed whole lambs (head included), platters of chicken, whole fish, beef, *pillo,* and salads and desserts in most imaginative designs. Even after the hundreds of us swarmed over the tables like hordes of locusts, there was still enough left for an army. It is part of the culture to have as much or more left over as is eaten. Policemen, servants, everyone working on the event, took over after the guests left. Always what is left is given to servants or to the needy.

It takes a lot of explaining—and I am sure it is never quite understood—why, in comparison, Americans have scant offerings of food at a dinner party. It is impractical to have a stack of steaks, for instance, left over to be reheated the next day, and we do not have the hordes of servants or others around to eat them. Even when I explained that often our leftovers end in a garbage disposal, I doubt if they felt that that was excuse enough.

UNGUIDED MISSILES

TAXI DRIVERS ARE IRAN'S UNGUIDED GROUND - TO - ground missiles. Their driving would make a racing driver blanch with envy, if not horror.

Traffic in Tehran is a serious problem, and for good reasons. In 1888 Tehran was a walled city, with a population of 150,000 people. Roads were not planned, and so were nothing but a hodgepodge. In 1927 Reza Shah replanned the city for 300,000 people, cutting new roads, putting in some pavement, and redesigning the city for better traffic. Nothing has been done since, although 1,800 buses were ordered a few years ago from Germany (the largest single order Mercedes Benz ever received) and there was no planning as to where they were to be used or who was to drive or maintain them. Imagine the added congestion!

This year, in addition to these same 1,800, many of which are in dilapidated condition, 175 double-decker buses were brought over from England. Their operation was launched amid much confusion. No one had considered the possibility of having to fell trees, change telephone wires and light poles to give them space. At first everyone was intrigued with the upper deck and rushed to sit there. Few ride there now; the passengers noticed there was no driver upstairs. They lost confidence.

To add to this bedlam, forty cars are added to the city traffic every day, so that at present there are 54,000 cars in Tehran, or a 900 per cent increase in twenty years. Of this number, 14,000 are taxis. This makes one car for every forty persons in a city that was originally planned to handle nothing but donkeys and camels.

Population has increased at the breath-taking rate of 100,000 persons per year. This means that there are two million people, including all suburbs, in a city planned for 300,000.

This bit of historical background is simply to explain why riding in taxis has become the quickest way to self-destruction in Tehran. There are laws, but the Persian, being the rugged individualist that he is, assumes they are made for the other fellow. Accelerated driving is the rule. Taxi fare is so low each passenger has to be quickly dispatched in order to have enough fares during the day and night to even pay for the rental of the machine. Fare anyplace in downtown Tehran had always been ten rials (about ten cents) until just recently when it jumped to fifteen rials.

Regular taxis are small, dilapidated foreign cars of ancient vintage. They are distinguished from private cars by their white-on-black license plates and white fenders, as against black-on-white plates of private cars. They always need repair. It is customary to drive a car or use any kind of machinery here without repairs until it falls apart.

Individual pride is not lacking, however, in the taxi decorations. Most have festoons of artificial paper flowers stuck in the windshield or dolls and gadgets dangling from the rearview mirror directly in front of the driver's eyes. One taxi, I recall, had the steering wheel done in sexy-looking mermaids, with the same subjects on every metal part of the interior, plus artificial flowers stretched around every window. And to top it all off, at night neon lights of every color blazed inside and out.

There is always a rush to get to the intersection ahead of everybody else. Usually two cars make it at the same time. Neither driver is willing to give so they sit it out. Fists are shaken, uncomplimentary remarks fly. Sometimes no one will move until traffic has lined up for blocks on both sides, and an intermediary takes over. If the intermediary is successful, so that neither driver loses face, it is possible to relieve the congestion.

Three cars abreast will often make the turn at an intersection at the same time, and cars from the right lane will turn left, or from the left lane will turn right, without warning or signal. Taxis pick up passengers in the middle of the street or wherever they happen to be.

It is only necessary to renew a driver's license every five years and up until about the time of our arrival they were secured more often with *bokshish* (bribe) than from examination. I am sure all the drivers with whom I rode wangled their licenses in this manner.

Certainly they didn't get them because they knew how to drive!

At least one man thought this should be an asset. His ideas on the matter appeared in the *Tehran Journal,* as quoted below:

TEHRAN — Speeding car hits and kills passer-by. Asked why he killed the man by crazy speeding, driver explains. "You see, I am not a skilled driver, haven't even got a license. So you see my offence is not as serious as that of a qualified driver."

The accident rate is very high. When accidents occur, crowds gather rapidly, and each person loudly expounds his version of what happened. The cars are left where the accident occurred until it is determined who is responsible. Sometimes a car will sit in the middle of the street for days while arguments rage between the parties and police. On such occasions it is necessary to hire someone to sit in what is left of the car to protect the remains from common thieves.

In my year as a regular taxi patron, I got more than my share of strange drivers. In fact, it seemed that eccentric drivers gravitate toward me. Among them was one who jerked his head from side to side, never varying the rhythm. This probably resulted from years of trying to look both directions at the same time to see where he was going to be hit next. Then there was the one who seemed hopped up with narcotics. He drove all ten miles on the wrong side of the street, missing by a hair's breadth hundreds of cars. Nobody but me batted an eyelash. Another one bodily swayed from side to side in a vain attempt to force his powerless car to carry me up the hill to Shimran. No wonder taxi driving is considered the most dangerous job in Iran.

I tried to select cabs which could make the grade up this gradual slope to Shimran. Each time I inquired if it could accomplish this feat, the answer was always "*Balle*" (yes) and the performance was usually "*Na*" (no). There were several times when the archaic model coughed out its last mile and left me stranded, clutching my armloads of groceries, then helplessly looking on as they fell through the bottom of the flimsy sacks.

After a few of these incidents, I came to realize that the group taxis (share taxis), which cruise from Shimran to Tehran and back, were the safest. They were larger and in better condition. Also the drivers were more careful. At least, you could share your anxiety with other passengers. It was a sure way of getting to rub shoulders with the populace! The legal limit is five passengers and the driver. My first experience in one of these taxis was almost my last. I rode with fourteen other people.

Our taxi was flagged down at the scene of an accident. Before I knew it there were two runny-nosed children on my lap, a fat mother who all but enveloped me along with herself in her *chador*, two dirty workmen with a loaded basket and tools on their laps, all of this and me on two jump seats. It had been some time since some people in the car had been to the *hamum* (bath). I couldn't see over the children, so I closed my eyes and let my imagination take over as we reeled from side to side. I managed to bruise myself quite evenly on all sides as I was plunged back and forth.

The experiences were never the same. One late afternoon, I shared the back seat with a pleasant, delightful, middle-aged man. The radio was blasting out dramatic Iranian music, as usual, loud and deafening. A voice came on and soared up and down the scale with great emotion. My seat mate noticed my struggle to catch the concept. In perfect English he translated.

"That's a Persian program beamed from Russia—in Persian. It is a beautiful description of the Utopian life of Russia. This is particularly about the fortunate little children who are taken from their mothers and put into the heavenly paradise of the communal schools. They are now describing them at play."

"Probably works both ways and puts the mother in paradise too, being separated from the little monsters all day," I laughed.

He smiled back and went on with the interpreting. It all built up into such a crescendo of perfection that I turned to the gentleman and said, "Shall we have the driver go right on over the border? A hundred miles isn't far. Never heard of life that ideal in any other place on earth."

"Nor I, and I spent twenty-five years in your country, in Washington, D.C., and I thought that was pretty good."

The gentleman was an executive in Plan Organization and had been in an important Iranian government position in the States. He was a fascinating conversationalist. When I got out he insisted on paying my fare. After some argument, he said, "I paid your son's fare last night, Mrs. Miller, so please permit me to pay yours today." I was left standing with my mouth wide open.

I stumbled the last block down our eroded *kutche* in complete bafflement, wondering how he knew my name. I had not told him.

Lloyd was at home. "Say, did you ride in a group taxi last night with a nice-looking Iranian man who spoke perfect English and paid your fare?" I quizzed.

He looked startled, "Paid my fare? Well, I took a group taxi after I taught my English class at the Iran American Society. Yeah, I did have a wonderful conversation with a smart guy about languages—but my fare—oh, no! I was so interested in what he had to say I must have forgotten to pay. Are they looking for me?"

"No, he just got through paying *my* fare. What I want to know is how he knew my name, and that I had a son? All I told him was that your father is at the university and that we live in California."

"That's simple. I told him the same two things, plus my name, and got off at the same stop. I told you he was smart. Great guy. We gotta find him and pay him back."

"I'd like to, but you know how Iranians are. I'm going to miss this gallant spirit of theirs when I leave."

Taxi drivers are not hired because of any knowledge of the city or streets. It is up to the fare to guide them. Only the main thoroughfares have names, and houses are all behind the same monotonous walls. Maps showing routes to friends' homes were given out instead of addresses, but it was a complicated game to follow them. The occasional house numbers are only for decoration—nothing else. Addresses are written as "First *kutche* past Plaza Hotel, second green gate on left." There were times when we rode for hours in search of a friend's home—without luck. A movement is under way to name the streets and number the houses. I hope I live long enough to see this.

After sixteen months we bought a car. We had been deterred by the fact that the driver alone is responsible in case of accident (not the owner), and the law is such that one could be put in a very desperate situation. I had vowed I would never drive—not one block —in Tehran. After several harrowing experiences, I ate my words, as I am usually forced to do, and started driving. Surprising how much safer one feels at the wheel, even though you might scare your friendly passengers half to death.

My years of driving in Los Angeles and on the freeways had prepared me somewhat for the experience. But not entirely. The first time I drove down Pahlavi from Shimran to Tehran I had the feeling that I was personally in charge of some mass suicide attempt. Every few feet one or more persons lay in wait for my approach, then dashed madly in front of my car or sauntered out as if there were no cars within a mile. I was to learn this was the rule. I was no more important to them than any other motorist.

I hadn't driven a car with regular shift since the automatic drives had made their appearance. This first

day, every time I went around a corner or made a
turn I would forget to shift, and there I would be
with the motor stalled and cars coming at me from
four directions.

That first mile could have been my last. As I cruised
prudently along in the deep concentration necessary
for survival in Tehran, two men from out of the blue
tossed a big Persian rug in front of the car. I slammed
on the brakes, turned out to miss it, almost killing a
pedestrian and just barely missing the car in front of
me, and came to a halt sideways after the car behind
me had grazed the back fender. I was raging mad at
the rug men. I looked back and they were shaking
their fists at me, motioning me to come back and run
over the rug. The idiots! That's the thanks I get for
saving their precious rug.

When I told Ali of this experience later that day
he doubled up with laughter. "They throw their rugs
out to be cleaned, and some to have them aged. The
reasons depend on who throws it. You are *supposed*
to run over them."

"Well, I can always say that the Persians threw
out the red carpet for me. It *was* red, too."

With my eyes closed, I imagined the chaos such a
stunt would create on a busy Los Angeles street.

Unnerved after that experience I crawled on down
the street as slowly as the bucking car would go, only
in the next block to have one of those exasperatingly
placid flocks of turkeys stroll into the path of my
car. I missed them.

Out of a hidden side *kutche* one of the king's horse-drawn water carts pulled in front of me. I had a rough time getting the car under control again. Bicyclists wove in and out without warning. Finally, I had to stop and get hold of myself before I dared proceed. I was even able to forgive the stupid donkeys for lurching in front of me, but I couldn't forgive their drivers who, being humans, should know better.

Eventually I sighted the turn on Takht-i-Jamshid which would lead me to the American Embassy where I planned to park the car so I could do my errands—on foot. This raised my spirits, but to reach my destination was not to be—yet.

A couple of jeeps roared by and signaled me to stop. Now what had I done? A look ahead gave me the clue. Down the street came what seemed to be the entire Iranian army heading "en masse" straight for me. Foot soldiers carrying rifles moved along in precision. Next came men walking beside horse-drawn heavy-caliber guns, then the cavalry, and after that blocks of overflowing jeeps with Tommy guns sticking out everywhere.

As they advanced closer and closer I shut my eyes. Surely their orders were to march straight through me and the car. As I dared to squint out of the corner of one eye I saw them side-step the car, neither looking left or right, without change of expression. It seemed that I sat there for hours reviewing the parade but it turned out to be only one hour. I kept worrying about what brought this all on. With all the revolutions and trouble raging around us, I thought this country must finally be in deep crisis. As soon as I was given the "go ahead" I had a frantic decision to make. Should I head for Sherm and the university, for home, or for the American Embassy? Common sense guided me to the Embassy; it was much the closest, and would be the safest in case of trouble.

As I was locking my car, two of my friends walked by.

"Say, you look pale. What's the matter?" asked Nelda Jessup.

"The army—did you see them—the whole darned Iranian army, and I got stuck right in the middle of it. Have you heard anything?"

"Oh, I know—that's the Azerbaijan practice parade. Don't tell me you got wound up in that performance? They go through that for days before the Shah reviews them at Jalalieh race track. Rehearse until they are absolutely perfect."

I went with my friends to the Embassy lunchroom. They easily persuaded me to go shopping by taxi. It was late afternoon when I set out for home.

As I turned onto Pahlavi, I couldn't believe my eyes! There was the same army marching the other direction. I didn't escape.

I tried after that to avoid driving into the Azerbaijan phalanx again, but the following week I went through it—twice—all over again.

Sherm bounced in happily shortly after I had dragged myself through the front door (after witnessing the last of my parades) and said, "Say, tomorrow is the big Azerbaijan parade. I knew you would want to see it so I got two tickets."

ROYAL RESORTS

THE NIGHT WAS DARK AND SOMBER, BUT THE AIR WAS fragrant and fresh at three o'clock in the morning. We tumbled out of bed and apathetically and mechanically dressed.

"I still don't see why we have to leave at this dreadful hour to go to the Caspian. Other people go at a decent time. Why is it imperative?" I complained drowsily.

"As I told you," Sherm answered, "Ali has had his car overhauled—new motor, and everything. It will be like breaking in a new car; travel at a snail's pace. The big climb over the Elburz Mountains would heat up the engine later in the day.

"I think he'll drive as usual, as fast as the car will go, new engine or not—nine-thousand-foot-high mountains, suicide curves, or not."

Ellen Lane, one of Marlene's friends, was going along and had spent the night with us. It was for talking, not sleeping, as proved by the difficulty we had rousing them.

However, we were actually ready, although not very bright, when we heard Ali's squeaky horn as he came plowing up the bumpy *kutche*. I cringed as I thought of the likelihood of his starting all the neighborhood dogs howling, the donkeys braying, and the roosters crowing.

He jumped out and met us at the gate. Cheerfully he began loading our luggage in the trunk, humming and singing his and our favorite popular Iranian song, "Maryam." Good-naturedly he grumbled, "Why do women always have to take so much junk?"

Many obstacles had been thrown in our paths since this trip was planned, and I was amazed that we had come this far. In the first place it was unbelievable that Ali's car had been finished as promised. Even he, used to Persians ways, didn't expect it.

Ali had picked up the car to try it out with a number of friends the night before. That same evening, Sherm and I were cruising home from a dinner party with the Bill Morgans when we were held up by a long line of stalled traffic.

Anything will collect a crowd in Iran, so we knew that the crowd was probably worse than the accident. That was the case. When we finally reached the center of activity, there we saw a car and taxi tangled in the middle of the street and at least seventy-five people milling around.

No dead bodies so it was nothing too serious, but there were the usual loud disputes and wranglings. One man was standing on the bumper inspecting the front of the rear car.

"Say, that guy looks like Ali," Sherm shouted as we slowed down.

"Sure enough, it is Ali." Ali had heard the commotion and caught sight of us immediately. Bill and Sherm piled out of our car to offer assistance.

Ali told us that a taxi had swerved in front of him from the wrong side of the street. He had done his best to avoid a bad accident, and had managed to finish with only a smashed grill and bumper.

The police arrived. More passionate, heated conversation. Ali pulled out his assortment of credentials. The police were properly and quickly impressed, and with many apologies and much bowing he was released. This saved him from spending his vacation in jail instead of at the Caspian with us.

Ali and Sherm had the car loaded and ready to go.

"Get in, everybody," Ali ordered.

I crawled into the back seat, put my pillow behind my head, and tried to go back to sleep. Everybody kept calling my attention to the fresh smell of the pure Tehran air and the fading stars that were blinking off one by one.

Even I had to admit it turned out to be a great idea, starting so early. We escaped the heavy traffic, which would have kept us in a cloud of dust on the rocky, unpaved mountain roads after we turned north from Karaj. The car chugged slowly along, and never once did the engine overheat.

The jagged, lofty peaks reminded us of the Rockies. Some of the passes are similar to those in parts of the Rocky Mountains, in Glacier National Park, and in Canada. This road is generally closed during the winter months. A few months after our passage an ava-

lanche killed many people and left the road impassable
for the rest of the winter.

We got to Chalus, first town of any consequence
on the other side, before noon. Chalus is famous for
its silk manufacturing. Aside from that, the people
make a scant living as tenant farmers.

It is here that the Caspian stretches from Iran to
Russia. "It is the largest landlocked body of water
in the world," Marlene reminded us. The gentle swells
are reminiscent of the Mediterranean and some of the
Florida beaches. The rainfall is about forty to sixty
inches, falling throughout the year, which gives it ex-
tensive marshes and dank jungle, and fertile fields of
rice, citrus fruits, melons, palm trees, and green lush
foliage. The population is more concentrated here along
the Caspian than in the rest of desert Iran. The dampness breeds unhealthy fevers but, thanks to Point Four
and the Iranian Ministry of Health, malaria has recently all but been eradicated.

"The best caviar in the world is brought out of
this sea. Expensive, but still half the price it is in the
States," Ali told us.

A spectacular example of railway building runs the
870 miles from the Persian Gulf to the Caspian. It
passes from sea level to 9,500 feet, crosses 4,102 bridges,
and goes through 224 tunnels, some of which cork-
screw inside the mountain.

Iran means "homeland of the Aryan," and most recent research indicates that the original Iranians mi-
grated south from the Caspian area. Since the formid-
able mountains have somewhat isolated them through

the centuries, their culture has remained pretty much unchanged. Some of these people are quite light in complexion. Their dress differs somewhat from that in the rest of Persia. Women wear long pants, short, gay, figured ruffled skirts falling just over their hips, men's vests over their shirts or blouses, and their *chadors* tied around their waists. Women carry heavy loads on their heads, poised on black skullcaps covered by white, flowing veils. They are usually barefoot and carry their babies tied to their backs.

Caspian men have the reputation of being very lazy. It is said women move south, if at all possible, to find males who will work and help support a family.

Houses built in the mountainsides have roofs of shakes or of used oil cans. In the fields, roofs and side walls are thatched, like those seen on the Hawaiian Islands. Many homes are on stilts because of the dampness.

On our way out of Chalus, Ali came to a sudden halt. We looked out and saw a lone, stately tree in the middle of a green field. Without a word, we all piled out—we knew we were going to have a picnic. Persians adore picnics and never go on a journey of any length without stopping several times, by a stream or under a tree.

Ali threw open the trunk of his car and pulled out his ever-present, finely woven Persian rugs and tossed them on the ground. Next came the samovar. We had purchased food from farmers and the villagers along the way.

"Hand me the fruit. I'll do the washing," Ali commanded as he stirred his solution of potassium per-

manganate and water. We washed the fruit thoroughly, poured sterilized water from his army jeep can
over it, and over our hands.

Along with the mixed Persian dried fruits and delicacies Ali had brought, we had fresh flaps of Persian
bread we had just bought at a village bakery, hot off
the pebbles, and cheese. Ali accompanied our lunch
with tales of Persia and his ever-ready proverbs. When
we got to the watermelon, we ladies tried to dispose
of the seeds delicately.

"Come on, be Persian. Have a good time. Spit them
out the way we do. When in Persia do as the Persians
do." Ali proceeded to show us how far he could spit
seeds. He looked like a champion.

From then on we had a wonderful time letting ourselves go, tossing manners as well as seeds to the winds.

It was time for the midday rest, so we took it right
there. Ingenious Ali fashioned pillows for the girls
and put down the back car seat for him and Sherm.
I had my own comfortable pillow.

Afterward we made our way to Ramsar, a famous
Caspian resort. Here, Reza Shah had built a magnificent hotel. We stayed there. The hotel is high on a
hill commanding a fabulous view of the sea. A prom-
enade, wide enough for two cars to pass, stretches from
the hotel terrace to the ocean, ending at a plush casino.
Landscaped gardens, in intricate designs, follow along
the sides of the entire walk. These same colorful, sym-
metrical gardens also surround the hotel. At night
the great artistry of this setting was transformed into
a fairyland of blazing lights.

Persian Picnic

After a few days of lolling on the beaches and floating in the sea at Ramsar, we drove on to Babulsar,
where there is another royal hotel built by the old
Shah. There are also royal summer palaces at Ramsar
and Babulsar.

In neither hotel are there elevators. Instead there
are impressive, winding staircases; we women felt like
queens and princesses as we paraded up and down on
the fine carpets.

Our rooms were cavernous at Babulsar. Deep rose
velvet draperies hung at our old-fashioned long windows. Overstuffed green chairs were set on delicate
maroon rugs. The spacious green tiled bathroom was
a surprise. The entire atmosphere made me feel as if
I were a participant in some Arabian Night's tale.

Meals were served in the garden. At night we danced
to a splendid orchestra which played our popular songs
and Persian music. Days were warm and languorous,
nights delightful.

After all the crowded beaches we have shared with
thousands, it was a real pleasure to find one with more
pebbles than people. At Babulsar we rented a make-
shift cabana. It was made of colored canvas strips tied
to stakes, with bamboo mats for lounging.

The beach crowd is primarily made up of men who
wear regular trunks and act like men everywhere in
the world. A strict Moslem woman will not expose
herself in public, or even at home, in a bathing suit.
Occasionally, we would see a not so strict one in the
crowd wearing a modest swim suit. They made it to
the water by racing down in their billowing *chadors*,

submerging themselves as quickly as possible, and then letting the *chador* float in to shore.

Returning to Tehran, we took the road on the other side of the mountains and went through the quaint village of Shahi. This side was a different world. There was Mount Demevend looking for all the world like Japan's Fujiyama with its snow topknot, guarding the rice paddies below.

"Japan, I swear it's Japan!" Marlene cried.

"It is, it is! See all the heavy forestation on the mountains? Exactly like Japan," agreed Ellen, who had lived there.

"Two worlds—this lush one here, and just a short distance away that granite, rocky, treeless land along the Chalus road," I said.

Ali commented, "See that old Demevend up there? That is mentioned in all kinds of our ancient stories about heroes and demons. We hear about that from the time we are little kids."

Our picnic experience was repeated, only with variations. This time we chose a lovely grassy meadow near a stream. We *thought* it was a grassy meadow. We climbed over a rickety fence made of scratchy boughs and barbed wire (I still have the scars) and slid down a precarious little hill. Ali had tossed the rugs over. Being a lady, I got to be helped across. I spread out one rug with myself on it, but before I was even settled I began to sink into what seemed to be quicksand but turned out to be a rice paddy. Marlene and Ellen flopped on the second rug before they realized my predicament—and immediately joined me

in the water. The men scrambled over just in time
to see us wading around, making strange noises as
we tried to rescue the rugs and ourselves. They grabbed
the rugs, tossed them back over, and did the same with
us dripping, muddy women.

"You know in Persia it's *'inshallah,'* 'if God wills.' "
Ali smiled.

Persians don't give up easily on the picnic idea. We
all moved to another clearing, carefully tested before
we ladies could be persuaded to try it.

Ali had insisted on buying a lamb from a sheep-
herder just out of Shahi. The cute little fellow was
in the trunk of his car. Marlene and Ellen insisted on
getting out every few feet, to open the trunk to give
him air and pet him. They thought he was going to
be a pet. Lambs, chickens, and turkeys are usually
bought on the hoof. They are cooked and eaten as
soon as they are killed. Iranians prefer their meat fresh.
They can't understand our keeping meat over a day.
Our frozen meat they would consider poisonous.

"Let's have one of those men over there in that
field kill the lamb." Ali pointed. "Then we can make
kebab on the little charcoal broiler.

"Oh, no, you can't kill that poor little innocent
lamb! Why, well—we would be cannibals if we ate
that little thing. You wouldn't really do that." Marlene was upset.

Ellen ran to the car and stood by the trunk to protect the lamb from slaughter.

Ali laughed. "Well, you eat meat killed by someone every day. What's the difference?"

"Well, it's just that—well, we aren't acquainted with the other animals, but this one is so darling—don't kill him—ever—please."

"O.K., if that's the way you feel about it. I'll go back to the last village and get some lamb already killed, and we can have kebab, anyway. It won't be any different, but if it will make you feel any better, I'll go." And that's where we got our lamb for the kebab.

Ali always kept the atmosphere strictly Persian with his Persian songs and high humor. We joined in with the ones we knew, and again forgot about Emily Post as we picked up our kebab with our fingers and ate with gusto and relish.

It took us five stops and three complete drainings of the radiator before our car made it to the summit. There were always plenty of other stalled cars to keep us company.

In Tehran we stopped at Ali's home to unload some of his belongings to make the car more comfortable for the ride to Shimran. Among the belongings was the gentle little lamb. The lamb followed us into the entrance hall, where he admired himself greatly in a large full-length mirror. It was with tears in their eyes that the girls left the little fellow, after smothering him with hugs.

The next day, Ali's driver was let in by our houseboy. He was bearing a large silver tray, on top of which was another large tray covered with a beautiful cloth. Ceremoniously he presented it to me. I peeked under the cloth, and there was a whole lamb ready for roasting.

We invited guests and had roast lamb the following evening. Somehow I wasn't hungry. Marlene said, "This is the best lamb we have had since we have been here. Why don't you have the cook go to this same place every time?" Then she regaled the guests with the story about a lamb Dr. Ali Azizi had bought for a pet.

SOAKED AND SOAPED

"Now let's be sure you have everything you need. Is it all right if I look into your—what you call it—bag?" Maryam Niami began checking through the suitcase I was taking. This was my first trip to the Persian bath.

"Large towel." She pulled out my beach towel, the largest I owned. "That's good. Two small towels, washcloth, head scarf, soap, hair shampoo, and—your comb, where is your comb?"

"Don't tell me I forgot that? Had it out there with my brush, all ready to bring," I apologized.

"It's all right. I give you one of mine—it's clean. If you not like that there is little store next to the bath where you can buy one."

"Good. I'll buy one at the little store. Can always use another comb."

"Then you have everything I told you to bring. I have all other things we need." She held up a bath mitt, "My mother had this made for you by one of her villagers. It is very special kind. You can't buy one like it. Notice, my dear, it is made of wool. I burned it all off myself—what you call it—you know those hairs of wool that are too long and would be bad for your skin, well, I wet the mitt, held it over the flame, and they went away—what you call that?"

" 'Singed,' I guess that's what you would call it."
She handed it to me and I rubbed my hand over it.
"Oh, I see. All the wooly feel is gone and it's so
smooth." This was a relief, as when she mentioned
wool I began to squirm. I couldn't imagine what that
would do to my sensitive skin.

It was Friday at the bath and what a crowd! Rooms
had been reserved for us, but even so, we had a short
wait. As we sat on our stiff chairs I watched the activity. Suitcases were piled high in the middle of the
floor of the waiting room, and the large red-striped
rough towels, worn by the men bath attendants, were
tossed in another heap. There were all kinds of people,
Persians, English, German, Dutch, and other nation-
alities not readily recognizable. This bath house was
run by a Zoroastrian; consequently, others besides Moslems were admitted. Many of the baths are strictly
for Moslems, and no non-Moslems would *dare* to enter.

"This bath is very high class. The very best one, I
think. For five years I come here and have the same
lady bathe me. You will have that one today," Maryam
Niami said.

"Since this is my first time, I would appreciate it
if you would tell me just what I am supposed to do."

"I think—this time—just this first time—you better
come with me. We will go into the same rooms. Always I have my own rooms, but today we go together."

When our number was called, we walked into the
rooms assigned to us. There was a small anteroom with
a bench of white tile along one side and a mirror on

the opposite wall. Being curious, I opened the next door and saw a large shower room with another bench. Just then a boy came in and threw potassium permanganate all over the shower-room floor and bench. Mrs. Niami waited until it met with her approval, then dismissed him.

I was poking my head in and out of doors. "Say, where is the pool we finally go into?"

"What you mean—the pool?" Mrs. Niami looked puzzled. "Oh, I know. We don't have pools in Tehran any more at bathhouses. We used to. Reza Shah had showers put in because they are more sanitary. In the villages they still have the pools. Those village people like it better that way, but it is hard to keep pools clean."

Without further explanation she opened her suitcase and got to work. She spread down a very unusual handmade mat on the tile bench, then on top of that a special heavy bath mat. "This is what we will sit on when we come out of the shower. Bring your soap, hair shampoo, washcloth, bath mitt, shower shoes, and follow me."

She unfolded a length of aqua-flowered cotton and wrapped around herself. "And where is your length of cotton?" she asked.

"I didn't have one, so I brought an extra towel instead." I quickly wrapped my towel around me and pattered behind her.

"I'll do everything first," she said.

She turned on the shower full force and began soaking her head and body, still wrapped in the length of

cotton. "Now, it's your turn." She motioned to me.
"Shall I leave the towel around me?" I inquired.

"Oh, my, yes, my dear. You must keep it on all
the time. Now that I have had this scrub attendant
for five years and she is used to me, I can take off
the material, but not in front of you. I would be embarrassed. You keep the towel around you all the time."

Since we were going to a dinner party that evening
it would not give me time to dry my hair, and since
I had a new permanent it would be impossible to manage without the aid of a hairdresser. I had brought
along my fancy shower hat made of feathers and se-
quins in floral patterns (sandwiched between two pieces
of plastic) with large gold earrings. One of my ever-
loving Stateside friends had sent it to me. It was a
most ingenious and pretty device for keeping hair day.

Mrs. Niami began to laugh. "What is that thing
on your head? Take it off. You must get your hair
washed. That is the best part."

"This is my shower cap. Can't get my hair washed
as I am going to a party right afterward. Next time."

Mrs. Niami looked aghast. "But with all the steam,
your hair will be no good! You have to get it washed.
Such a wonderful scrubbing they give you. Take off
your hat."

I had told Sherm that nobody, not even the determined Persians could get me to wash my hair this
time. He had said, "Well, I don't know, but we will
see who wins—you or the Persians."

The attendant bounced in. What a metamorphosis!
Mrs. Niami had pointed her out to me in the wait-

ing room. She was a shapeless, nondescript woman concealed in a *chador* with long pants hanging below. I wondered if she would wear that outfit when she scrubbed us. Somehow, I was rather shocked to see her standing there nude, except for a pair of well worn, baggy underpants. I discovered Persian females look the same out of *chador* as other women.

Without a word she snatched off my prized shower cap and shoved me beneath the shower. It was obvious I would be having my hair washed after all. While I showered and showered, she gave Mrs. Niami her shampoo. Soon it was my turn.

I handed her my shampoo, and she vetoed it. Mrs. Niami gave her some of her special soap for me and explained, "You can have your shampoo at the last, but it will make your skin too slick as it will run down on it, and then she can't scrub you well."

The attendant bore down and went to work on my head like an Olympic trainer working on the calves of a long-distance runner. Soap was running all over my face and body, and although I kept my eyes tightly shut, I could feel the sting of it. A vessel of water was suddenly poured over me, I gasped for breath and had a sensation of drowning. Just caught my breath in time to be deluged again, and this time I came up gurgling. Came up for a big breath of air and got my bearings in time to be drenched, then saturated and left choking.

She scoured away as if this would be the first and last shampoo of my life. I thought it definitely would be my last; I was sure I wouldn't have a hair left on my head. Or I would be pronounced dead from drowning. As I contemplated this possibility, the flood came again, and again. Then, when I was trying to get enough air to scream "uncle," I was inundated for the last time, and somebody was taking me by the hand, leading me somewhere. A torrent suddenly hit me on the head, and I knew I was back under the shower.

At this point I had completely forgotten about the towel that had been draped around me. Evidently it lost its moorings, as I could hear faint squeals from Mrs. Niami through my soap-filled ears and the rush of the shower.

"Your towel—it is falling. Quick, grab it," she called desperately.

I flailed the air trying to seize it, but being unable to open my eyes, I had to do it by feel. I caught it just as it slid to my navel and saved us both from calamity. With one hand clutching the towel to keep me from appearing stark naked, I tried to wash out the soap in my hair and use the comb, as instructed, at the same time. This operation would take three hands.

"Maryam, why don't you turn around, so I can use both hands?" I pleaded.

"Oh, no! Please—keep the towel around you."

"It's come untied. It won't stay," I lamented.

"I will fix it, I will fix it." She jumped up from whatever stage of the process she was in and tied the towel securely around me.

Mrs. Niami had brought along a tray each for us to sit on, so we would not run any chances of picking up stray microbes. Her late father had been a famous Iranian doctor and Minister of Health, which would account for her being so germ-conscious.

I still couldn't get my eyes open. In trying to sit on my tray I missed it, and the tray and I clattered to the floor. There I was, sprawled out on the slippery tile. Mrs. Niami and the attendant pulled me to my feet and threw disinfectant over my bottom to ward off any germs I may have contacted.

"The herbs are here ready for our hair. Most all ladies use henna, as you know. These herbs are just as good for your hair, but have no color."

"Why do so many people use henna?" I asked.

"The henna you see on the third-class citizens used to be used on their hands and hair to make them beautiful, but also they use it now like a disinfectant. They use it on the soles of their feet, too. On the donkeys and animals it is to make them pretty. They use it on children and everybody."

"Yes, everywhere I go I see henna-haired youngsters as well as mothers and grandmothers, and even old men, their hair and their beards henna-colored," I said.

Through my blurry eyes I could see a powdery substance which she stirred with water into a light gelatinous mixture. This was worked into my hair, then the shampooing started all over again. Under the shower, then down to the business of the body scrubbing.

I looked over at Mrs. Niami as she was being scrubbed with the mitt, and there she was looking just like that old cliché and nothing else, "a boiled lobster."

I wondered what would happen to poor me, who

was not accustomed to it. I soon found out. The skin rolled and flaked off all over the bench. Mrs. Niami showed me how her skin had done the same thing and told me how delighted the attendant was that mine was coming off so well.

"Usually, the first time it doesn't respond that well," Mrs. Niami explained. "She rubbing too hard?"

"So far I can stand it."

Every inch of my body was relieved of its weary, worn-out skin. I felt my arms and they were just like the ads, "the skin you love to touch."

Pumice stone was used on our feet. Then our hair and bodies were rinsed again for several minutes under the shower. We were pronounced clean. The attendant vanished.

Mrs. Niami handed me an egg.

"What's this for?"

"We will now give ourselves a face mask. Put your hand in it and mix it well—see like this." She demonstrated. "Then rub it carefully all over your face, your neck, and breasts; the white of it we will put on the rest of our bodies. This is full of vitamins and very good for the face."

I eat eggs only because I think I should and have a miserable time trying to choke them down, and then only if I don't have to look at them. I warily looked into the special little dish she had brought for me, and reluctantly began to stir. My hand slithered around in that gooshy egg yolk, while I tried not to look. My stomach did a few nip-ups, and for a minute I thought I couldn't go through with it. I told myself I had overcome all of that silly squeamishness, closed my eyes, and rubbed the mess all over my face.

"Now, we sit down and rest while this dries. When it is very dry, then we wash it off, take another shower, then all over our face and body we put these creams I have brought. Then we are finished." Finished—that was the word to describe me right now!

After another shower (I had long ceased to count them) I was pronounced finished and sent to the ante-room to sit on the carefully laid-out mat.

Mrs. Niami unwrapped a bundle of the same floral pattern as the length of material in which she was wrapped. Inside were beautiful, heavy aqua towels, same color as the background of the floral material, deliciously fragrant with Persia's famous rose water.

We gave ourselves a complete facial, after which Mrs. Niami drenched me and herself with rose water, and said we were through.

The entire procedure had taken two hours, and with all the steam and scrubbing and water, I was really exhausted.

I could barely make it to the car. Sherm was wait-ing, and when he saw my head all done up in a cotton scarf (borrowed from Mrs. Niami), he began to laugh.

As I got in, he mumbled, "I see the Persians won," then out loud, "Wow! You look clean, really clean."

"I am!" and this was an understatement.

When we got home, I dried my hair as best I could and tied on my most attractive scarf. My permanent kept springing up and standing on end all around my head.

When I first took off the cotton bath scarf Sherm roared, "Talk about a Zulu native. Have you seen yourself in the mirror?"

No doubt people at the party thought it rather odd that I wore a scarf all evening with a cocktail dress, and dozed in a chair most of the time. I told my hostess that I had been to the bath, but didn't have the strength to make explanations to the others.

Never had a sounder night's sleep, and the next day there was not a trace of red skin. It was velvety and soft with hardly a freckle left. Glad I hadn't worked all summer for a good sun tan, because this would have been the end of it. From this day on I became a confirmed Persian bath enthusiast.

IRAQ COUP

IT WAS A DELIGHTFUL JULY NIGHT. OUR SPIRITS WERE high in anticipation of a festive evening, dining and dancing at the Darband Hotel. The Niamis, Ali, and other Iranian friends were accompanying us.

Just before they came Sherm was called to the telephone. "No! This can't be true! No warning of any kind—nobody knew—no leak about the plot? I hate to mention it, but I just said to Max the other day, Baghdad would probably be the next trouble spot with Lebanon, Jordan, and Egypt all getting into the act. You remember, we were there only a month ago, and at that time we were particularly impressed with how well off they appeared. They were making much more progress than any other country we saw in the entire Middle East."

Straining at Sherm's elbow, I kept interrupting, "What is it—tell me—what has happened?"

Sherm went on into the phone, "I just can't believe it. Say, this doesn't look good, does it? Why, never heard of anything so gruesome — that's right down medieval! Excuse me just a minute—Maxine is here heckling me."

With a grim expression he turned to me. "It's Iraq —*coup d'état*—army turned on King Feisal and Nuri el Said. King's own soldiers killed him—wiped out his entire family and Nuri el Said. Mob went crazy, dragged them through the streets, tore them limb from limb, hung them from lampposts, cut off their feet. It's too terrible to talk about."

Sherm went back to his conversation with Colonel Carter. In my heart I knew if it could happen to our neighbor it could happen anywhere, anytime.

"What does this mean?" I asked, sickened, as he hung up the telephone.

"It means that nobody knew what was going on except the plotters. They were so clever they took the whole world by surprise. Makes you feel insecure anyplace. It's incredible! They ambushed them all at the airport while they were waiting for the plane to Istanbul—they were going to attend the Baghdad Pact meeting."

"Oh! What do you think has happened to Sarah and Abbas—and Dr. Jamali?"

Sarah Jamali is Sherm's cousin, who, as a young lady twenty-five years ago, left her happy, comfortable home in Minneapolis to teach in Baghdad.

As she had told us, just a month before, when we were guests in her charming home in Baghdad, "I found that I could adjust to any country and customs after my year's experience. The next year I married Dr. Jamali. We had met at Columbia University when we were both graduate students and had become very dear friends there. I have remained here since, except for an occasional trip to Europe and the States. I have had a wonderful and rewarding life. These are now my people and there are so many more things I hope to do to help them."

She and her son Abbas, aged fifteen, had returned our visit, and after ten days with us in Iran had left only four days ago. The anxiety of this latest situation in Iraq consequently hit very close to our hearts.

"Dr. Jamali is in New York now, according to what Sarah said. He is the Iraq representative at the Security Council, so he is safe," Sherm assured me.

"He is such a rabid nationalist, surely they wouldn't do anything to him, anyway," I reflected. "They will never find another man as understanding, interested, and devoted to his people. The Jamalis live so differently than most people would in their position—so simply and unpretentiously. Remember how busy he was—people coming and going for conferences—still he took time out to answer our questions patiently and discuss Middle Eastern events with us."

Sherm said, "All his life he has been in government service when he could have had any number of more lucrative jobs at home or abroad. Now, let's see—he was prime minister twice—foreign minister seven times —president of the Chamber of Deputies twice, and chairman of the Iraqi delegation to almost every session when they participated at the meetings of the Arab League."

"I found Sarah Jamali to be a very remarkable person. After twenty-five years in Baghdad she lives and thinks exactly like an Iraqi and speaks the language as well as a native. Being the intellectual that she is, the self-effacing humanitarian, I don't think she would have been happy leading an ordinary American house-wife's existence," I said.

While she was our guest, her mind never left her people. She graciously turned down all social engage-ments and parties in favor of concentrating on the native handicrafts of Iran. She wanted to take new skills back to her peasants. She spent the rest of the time conferring with heads of women's clubs here to see if they had any new philanthropic ideas which were practical for Iraq.

As we were talking, we heard Ali's signal, the familiar horn.

Heavy silence greeted us after a forced try at a jovial "Good evening" as we took our seats in the car. We knew he must have heard the news.

After about a mile up Pahlavi, Ali ventured, "Some-thing pretty serious has happened in Iraq."

"Yes," said Sherm. "We just heard about it. What's the implication for Iran?"

"Don't know—have no idea."

"It doesn't seem possible that human beings can be so cruel and barbaric," I put in. "Such cold-blooded killings and draggings of the bodies through the streets is beyond my comprehension! Who said this world is civilized?"

Ali countered, "We have had so much of this through the centuries that maybe in this part of the world we don't feel the way you do. Actually, if you are going to overthrow a government, you have to wipe it all out or it will rise up again."

We didn't want to talk about it any more. Sherm

and I just listened to the observations made by the Niamis and Ali. They had differences of opinion.

"What will happen to Americans if anything like that occurs in Iran," I asked.

"Nothing."

But I was not convinced.

The following evening, while I was waiting for Sherm to come from his Board of Directors meeting at the American Club, Ali came to take us to one of his many cousins' wedding receptions. He had brought along the Persian evening paper and began translating the news to me, as was his custom when he came to visit.

Immediately I noticed a picture of Dr. Jamali. I couldn't read the article, but I began demanding that he start with that. Ali took one look, let out a gasp, and said, "They are moving troops to the Persian Gulf."

"Is that pretty bad?" I asked. "But please tell me what it says about Dr. Jamali. I can't stand the suspense."

Calmly he read on. "He has been replaced in the Security Council by another man."

"Is that all it says?"

"Read it yourself if you don't believe me." He smiled sheepishly.

"I have to believe you—no alternative."

Sherm rushed in and called, "Max, Dr. Jamali——," but before he could finish, Ali jumped up to meet him, yelling as he went, "Yes, he has been kicked out of the Security Council." From the rear I could see him wildly gesticulating.

I remained on the terrace, and they both came back out talking about something else.

I asked Ali, "Do you think we could possibly get any word to Sarah Jamali? You remember her. You met her when she was here."

"I wouldn't try just now if I were you." With that he gave Sherm a knowing look.

The next day I heard over Voice of America what Ali had struggled so diligently to keep from me— that Dr. Jamali had met the same fate as the king— and his body had also been dragged through the streets. After days of distress, this report proved to be false —he was alive, but had been taken prisoner. His only words were, "I am as much a Nationalist as you are." This was his statement to the soldier as he was led off to prison.

I appreciated Ali's keeping the news from me; it would have been a great shock coming so suddenly. When I said to him, "That was most considerate of you," he replied, "It is too much for women to hear these things all at once. They must be told a little at a time. They must be prepared. My favorite brother was run over by a bus and killed when he was twelve. The three of us brothers were going to the Caspian for a holiday. My brother got out of the car to buy something for us, and when he started back to the car, a bus crossed into the wrong side of the road and crushed him to death. It was a terrible thing and I will never, *never* forget that sight! For two months our father kept the two of us who were living hidden in a home in Tehran and each day prepared our mother for the news of the tragedy. He pretended we were still at the Caspian but that our younger brother was a little bit sick—at first. Each day he would become sicker. Then my brother and I would write letters, and they would be taken to the Caspian and mailed back to Tehran to mother. After weeks, when mother realized that my brother could not recover and her mind was ready, then my father told her the truth."

"Wasn't she anxious to go to your brother all that time he was supposed to be ill?"

"Every day she wanted to go. That made lots of trouble for my father. Every day he would need to have a new excuse why she couldn't go. My father loved my mother with every cell in his body. He could never bear to see her hurt. Theirs, of course, was an arranged marriage. She was fourteen and he nineteen. Oh, how they learned really to love each other! It was wonderful and beautiful." I detected a misty film over his deep, expressive eyes.

On the way home, we stopped in at the American Club to call for Marlene and get a late snack. The radio was blasting out the news on Voice of America. We were joking and laughing at a table with friends when the news came over that the Russians were moving down toward the Iran border. The details sounded as if they were ready for business. No one commented except one of Marlene's friends who came up and said, "Well, how's your Russian?"

"Not good enough," Marlene replied. Slowly, one

by one, without open signs of panic, we left the club
to go home and pack our evacuation bags.

Ali assured us all the way home that if it were in
his power, no harm would come to us, and that if
necessary he would take us to his village, which was
so remote nobody could ever find us. This gave us
some comfort, although, practically speaking, it would
probably have been impossible to get out of the city
if there were trouble. We hoped the Embassy was well
prepared for us, although up to now, nothing had been
said as to where we should go in case of an emergency.

Next morning we were up early trying to get the
news on Voice of America, but Radio Moscow was
jamming, as usual, so we heard only their slanted reports. We felt our beautiful world quickly slipping
from under us but tried to be optimistic, and with
our great friend Ali encouraging us, we were able to
make a good pretense. His concern was as great as
ours, I am sure, but never once did he allow himself
the luxury of showing it.

These events took place just as we were coming into
the month of Moharram, Islam's month of mourning.
Emotions run very high at this time, especially against
foreigners. Americans were advised to remain inside
their homes on the four deepest mourning days. Special
notices went out to all of us that no radios, phono-
graphs, or musical instruments of any kind should be
played, no parties given, and no cameras taken out
of the house. "Do not attract any attention to yourselves in any way," they said. This added to the anxiety
among us.

Islam is divided into the two main sects—Shi'a and Sunnite. In Iran, Turkey, Egypt, and wherever Shi'a communities exist, this month is observed.

At this time the pathetic and lamentable story is enacted of the calamity of Hossein, the grandson of Mohammed. The two Moslem sects came into being when there was a schism over leadership. Ali, cousin, and son-in-law of Mohammed, became leader of the Shi'a sect.

Hossein was urged by his adherents to assert his right to the Caliphate in A.D. 680. So he, along with his party of thirty armed men on horseback and forty on foot, accompanied by their wives and children, set off across the desert for Kufa, near Baghdad. The little band was attacked outside the city by foreigners (that's why feeling runs so high at this time against foreigners). Fighting desperately, the seventy refused to surrender, even though they were without water. They were cut down one by one, until only the women were left. All the families were taken captive. Not even the children were spared.

The city of Kerbela, in Iraq, has grown up around the shrine of Hossein. Here, in life, the Shi'as perform their pilgrimages, and here, before death, they make provision, whenever possible, to be buried.

The two Arabic months of Moharram and Safar usually fall somewhere in July and August. The first ten days are of deep mourning, the ninth and tenth (Tassoua and Ashura) are most important of all.

Temporary mosques are set up in every neighborhood where the Miracle Play (*ta'zieh,* re-enactment of

Hossein's tragedy) is given all during the month. On the deepest mourning days, men fanatics parade through the streets, beating their breasts, sometimes practicing self-mutilations with knives and chains, while chanting tirelessly in wailing cadence the mourning cry of "*Ya Hassan, Ya Hossein.*" From our roof top, in the dark of night, we secretly watched these parades of men, stripped to the waist, or in black shirts open at the back so as to leave the bare flesh exposed for beating. Some faked wounds with ketchup or similar concoctions, while the wounds on others were very real. Heads were bandaged. Others left scars for all to see. Some were hired to suffer for those who found it easier to do it vicariously. Some were repenting and doing it for their own emotional satisfaction. We never knew if Doran and Mohammed joined in the parades, but they wore black shirts the entire month, went to the passion plays, and sustained an abject and woebegone countenance the whole time.

One of the mosques was set up just a block from our home. Far into the night we heard the mournful wailing and chanting, night after night. We could hear the audience screaming "*abe*" (water), "*khon*" (blood) and other climactic words as the drama progressed. It was not possible for a foreigner to witness these performances unless he wished to live dangerously. The upper-class Iranians, who wore coats and ties, would not have dared to attend unless they could masquerade as lower class citizens, since the assembly was made up of these people.

This would have been a propitious time, with emotions already fanned to a frenzy, to incite the lower classes to any kind of internal violence.

The emotion - packed atmosphere was electrified. What a time for agitation!

Moharram's last day dawned, much to our relief, without incident. Little by little the tension eased. Rumors were always flying, but on the surface the *status quo* continued.

We tried in every way to learn the whereabouts of Sarah and Abbas. We knew Dr. Jamali was in jail and eventually learned from the newspapers that they put him through a phony trial and, as stated in *Time* magazine, "With dignity and courage he defended himself. The sentence: death by hanging. On hearing the verdict, Jamali seemed almost to lose his balance, then leaned wearily on the railing of the prisoner's box." We couldn't reconcile this scene with those in which we had participated with him.

We tried by several methods to contact Sarah, but without success. About six months after the revolution a most welcome letter came through from her via the States. With great understatement she apologized for not writing us sooner, but, she quoted, "man proposes and God disposes." She told us that her telephone had been torn from the wall by the rebels, and she mentioned, with her delightful sense of humor, "I thought of wrapping up the telephone directories, which they left behind, and sending them to the government with my compliments, but reluctantly gave up the idea." Her letter continued, "In desperation and casting around for a place of refuge, as it was unsafe to remain in my own home, we entered a home and asked to use the telephone in the hope of finding some relative's or friend's home where we could go. Telephone lines had been disconnected to many homes, so communication was limited. Although we were complete strangers, we were welcomed there to stay with these hospitable Americans." (The first news of the Jamalis was brought out of Iraq by this family when they were evacuated to the States.)

"I was sure that our many friends were thinking about us and praying for us," she wrote. "And I was so thankful for God, the great Coordinator, who can take thoughts and deeds and wishes of people who have no means of communication and combine them into a power for good that extends throughout the Universe. Believe me, we are never alone.

"During the days when hate was released and freed in our streets, when fear and the instinct of self-preservation were uppermost in the lives of everyone, and the name Jamali was a liability, I met the most amazing care, kindness, and courtesy from relatives, friends, and strangers.

"One outstanding example was our dear old woman servant, you remember her, Daughter of Senile. In spite of my telling her to leave our house and go to the safety of her relatives, in spite of what she heard and saw, and in spite of the general hysteria, she stayed on in our house alone for a month until we returned. What amazing love and loyalty."

This brought the picture of that old servant to my mind. She had no other name than "Daughter of

Senile" and had been with them since they were married.
I could see her as she startled us our first morning
by appearing at the breakfast table clothed in native
black Bedouin dress, balancing a huge silver tray full
of food on her head, her black head covering flowing from underneath the tray. She had tattoo marks
on her arms, hands, and around her mouth—her beauty
marks.

To continue Sarah's letter: "On July 14 in the morning when I came down off the roof, where I had been
sleeping, I found Fadhel, not yet ready to leave for
the airport to accompany H.M. King Faisal to Turkey
for the Baghdad Pact meeting. I said, 'What's the matter? Aren't you going to be late?'

"He said, 'Listen to the radio. There's a *coup d'état*.'

"I listened to a raucous, hysterical voice announc-
ing the overthrow of the old government and the for-
mation of a new one, with two army men in charge.

" 'Well,' I said, 'they haven't arrested you yet; the
way is open, so get going.' He took his passport, and
left. Later we heard that he had been killed, which
I refused to believe. (It was a case of mistaken ident-
ity. Some other poor fellow had met that dreadful
fate.)

"Then on the third day, Fadhel was arrested on a
farm outside Baghdad. The mobs were fierce and were
looking for him, so he wouldn't have had a chance in
Baghdad.

"We have been allowed back in our home. All of
our assets have been frozen.

"As for Fadhel, the wheel has made a complete circle.

As a boy and son of a religious sheik, he was destined to study religion in a theological school, but he rebelled and entered the first teacher training school in Iraq. Now, he is spending his time in a cell, he prays five times a day, and reads the Koran. He is learning Kurdish from a fellow prisoner.

"I hope they will allow me to continue working to help the deserving people at Ramzi School. My spirit is quite sturdy and strong. How thankful I am—so thankful to be able to hand over the past and the future to God, and to take His guidance for only one day at a time. It is enough."

Looking back on our delightful days, visiting together on our terrace in the peace and quiet of our Persian garden, I thought of the dreams she had confided to me for the underprivileged people of Iraq, and of the tremendous progress which was being made at that time. We had discussed philosophy, and especially the Koran. Abbas was well versed in it and was a strict and devout Moslem. Already he had a most wonderful and workable philosophy of life, and his knowledge of world politics was incredible for a boy so young. From him and his mother, I had received a profound education. How were we to know that within four days' time their world would be shattered and ours threatened? (At this writing, Dr. Jamali has finally been released from prison, and is living quietly with his wife in Iraq.)

LES GIRLS

THERE WAS THE CLANGING OF THE GATE. ALI emerged, wrestling a live turkey, with Doran shuffling in behind.

"Do you want him killed right now or keep him as a pet for a while?" Ali was trying to maintain a tight grip on the turkey's feet, as it squirmed around, glaring with its reddened eyes.

"My gosh, Ali, you don't expect us to kill that thing, do you?" Sherm reached out to take it and got a wing in his eye for his trouble.

"Of course, I don't expect *you* to kill him—just give him to Mohammed—he will do it."

I hesitatingly added, "Thanks so much." I never knew whether Ali was throwing these situations at me to test my ability to cope with them, or not. This was the latest of several live turkeys he had generously given us.

The first experience with live birds occurred when I was not at home. Marlene and her friend, Ellen, were listening to records when Ali's driver appeared at the gate with a flapping turkey. It was Doran's day off, and not knowing what to do with the bird, they dashed out to Mohammed and urged him to do something—quickly. Acting promptly at their request, he chopped off its head and brought it back into the house. Since it had not quite perished, the determined fowl demonstrated his persistence to live by running headless up and down the halls. As it was told to me, the girls ran screaming back and forth trying to chase it into the kitchen where they hoped to corner it— but they had no luck. Mohammed was drafted into the chase, and with much Persian hubbub and physical dexterity, he cornered it. These gymnastics didn't alter the taste of the old bird a bit. When it reached our dining table it was delicious.

Acting on these past experiences, my urgent ring brought Mohammed on the double, and when he took in the situation, he grabbed the turkey and vanished like grease from under a hot iron.

"He's onto your ways, Ali. Didn't have to make any explanations. Come on in the living room. Good to see you. Doran, bring coffee," Sherm ordered.

"Please sit down." I gestured. "We were hoping you would drop by. What's new?"

"Quite a bit," Ali answered as he handed his coat to Doran, then sat down with us. I detected that mischievous twinkle and noted that self-conscious little smile. He had something very much worth telling, if we could persuade him to talk.

"Come on, Ali, tell us. What is it? Another girl?" I was only making a stab in the dark.

"That's right." He smiled, then laughed right out loud when he saw my surprise.

"Imagine my being right for once," I said as I moved my chair closer, my ears expanding in anticipation.

"There you are, just like a woman with your ears flapping."

"That's right. Hurry up and tell us. Now, is this *really* serious this time?"

"Well—I'd say—somehow serious. After tonight it will probably be 90 per cent serious. I'll start from the beginning. You know my best friends, Hamid and his wife Yasmin? Well, they are—what you call it— uh—broker—go-between—you know what I mean. A month ago Yasmin came to see my mother to tell her about this girl who is a friend of hers. I came home when she was telling her all about it, and it sounded pretty good. Excellent family, girl about twenty-two —good age—speaks English, not too bad looking. So —we made arrangements for me to get a look at her in the department store—you know—Forushgahe Ferdowsi.

"I was supposed to be at the store at 10:30 in the morning, so I got there at 11:30. Hamid was out front pacing up and down. He was upset because they had waited a whole hour, and the girl and her mother were about to leave. He said if I hurried I could see them; they were still drinking tea in the tearoom."

"Why were you late?" I inquired.

Ali grinned, and those little demons flickered again in his black eyes.

"Oh, oh—I know—indifference for effect," I accused, but he didn't answer—just went on with the story.

"We walked into the tearoom and sat down with Hamid's wife. They showed me where the girl and her mother were sitting and asked me to move to their

Ali Talks Turkey

table. I insisted that we invite the ladies to our table, but after much argument, Hamid said it would be more gallant if we accepted the invitation of the ladies—it would look better for them. So that's what we did. I talked with the mother about general things and looked —just a little bit—at the girl."

"Say, tell us—was she pretty?" I was terribly interested.

Ali hesitated. "Well—she wasn't beautiful, but I guess she was kind of pretty."

"Pretty enough?" Sherm wanted to know. Ali's idea of the perfect wife was the concept most typical of all the Iranian men we had met—beauty came first, then the right family was next. I never heard any other qualifications stressed very much.

"Well, I think so—she wasn't as beautiful as I would like, but I think she is all right. We had tea with them, then I excused myself and left. Yasmin arranged for me to have tea at the girl's home the next week. I went to her home, and there were several of her father's gentlemen friends whom I knew, so I turned my back on the ladies so they couldn't stare at me, and talked with the men. The girl was passing cakes and all those little things, but I never looked at her —never saw her at all this time."

"How did you take the cakes without looking at her?"

"I just kept my eyes down on the plate, that's all."

"You aren't very inquisitive. I should think you would want to get a good long look. Why did you put on this disinterested act?"

"Believe me, it was not an act. You just don't know how hard it was for me with all the servants peeking through the curtains, and everybody looking at me. I could feel all those eyes on me. It was horrible! The sweat just rolled off me. This time I didn't stay very long."

"You're really Western, getting to see her all of two times. Why, you are a regular reprobate," I teased.

"That isn't all—I've seen her *three* times. Hamid and his wife arranged a tea at their home. I thought, maybe they could plan for me to have a few words with her then. I wanted to ask her what she is like and tell her all about what I am like. This is very much against tradition, and I haven't been able to do this—yet. Her family is very modern, but not modern enough for me to be left with her even for a minute, or even to converse, just the two of us, in the family group. But I have one other chance to speak to her, alone perhaps—and that's tonight."

"You mean now, soon?"

"Tonight in—" he looked at his watch, "a couple of hours. Her family is having a big dinner party for all their important friends—and me. The girl's aunt called me directly, didn't go through Yasmin. This is not traditional, as they are supposed to contact me through the go-between, but they claim this party has nothing to do with the marriage negotiations. Just a little get-together, they said. Of course, I know better. If I go tonight this will be"—he hedged—"what you say—you know what's the word—finish———"

"Clinch it?" I supplied.

"Yes, that's it, clinch it."

"After tonight you can't change your mind?"

"Not very well. It will have gone too far. Believe me, I'm getting pretty nervous. I want to talk to the girl at least once before it is all settled—but then again, I don't want to. I don't like to have too much break with tradition for the sake of my mother."

"Oh, this *is* something. Will you bring the girl over to meet us as soon as you can?"

"Probably not the girl, maybe her brother or someone in her family. Well, I don't know—maybe even the girl with some of her family," he fidgeted.

I rang the bell for Doran to give Ali a respite and chance to try to relax while he waited for more coffee.

Ali glanced again at his watch, took out one of his miniature Iranian cigarettes, lit it, and began to puff furiously. As the time for the party drew closer, he became more uncertain of everything by the minute.

"Seems to me this is a pretty cold and unromantic way of getting into a marriage," Sherm intervened. "Now, if you don't like what you see tonight, why don't you just drop the whole thing and start over with some other girl?"

"You don't understand. It isn't that easy."

I didn't want them to argue the point. "Will you call us tomorrow and tell us what happened? This is getting exciting."

"I'll come and take you to lunch at the Darband Hotel and tell you all about it then."

At nine o'clock the same evening, our telephone rang. I answered. It was Ali. His voice was almost inaudible.

"Ali, good heavens, are you at the party?" I hollered into the mouthpiece, hoping my loud voice would stir some animation in his.

"No, I'm home," came back a feeble reply.

"Why aren't you at the party?"

"Give me a chance to tell you. My uncle, my mother's brother—that would be my uncle, wouldn't it—well he is very sick. When I stopped by my house on the way to the party, my mother had left a message that under the circumstances I should not go. It is not customary to be out having a good time when a member of the family is seriously sick—so—I did not go to the party."

"Oh, that's a shame!" I felt let down, so what must he have felt? "This won't close the door on it, will it?"

"I don't know. It depends on lots of things."

"Did you get word to them that you aren't coming?"

"Yes. I called Hamid and he had his wife call them."

"Come on back up and visit with us some more. Maybe we could go someplace, help you get your mind off your troubles."

"Thanks, but all I want to do now is get some sleep. I'm exhausted! Now, there won't be any story to tell you tomorrow, but I'll come and take you to lunch anyway."

"O.K. We will make up our own narrative. How's that?"

We hung up, and I relayed the disappointing news to Sherm.

Next day, when Ali came, he surprised us with spectacular Kashghai tribal costumes he'd had made to order for us in Shiraz. It was fun putting them on, and Ali agreed that we would make very acceptable tribespeople, with just a little more weathering of the skin. There was much bantering in a light vein, and we purposely avoided asking him questions, until Sherm did eventually venture, "How is your uncle?"

"Not expected to live. Probably won't last out the night. It's all right, though, if we go to lunch. Come on, let's go. Will help to get my mind off everything."

It was Friday and the hotel was crowded with happy groups dressed in their very best.

Kebab (barbecued lamb) is a favorite with Iranians and with us as well, so we ordered that.

Purposely, we talked about many unimportant things.

"So I guess that girl and her family were pretty upset when I couldn't go to their party last night," Ali finally said.

"What did they say?" I shot back.

Ali shook his head slowly with emphasis. "Wow! I guess it was awful. Hamid's wife said they didn't think that was the real reason and slammed up the phone in her ear. Oh, she was furious. She was *so* mad! She was glad that I didn't go. She said it served them right for dealing directly with me instead of through her, since she started the whole thing. She told them now they could see what happened to their secret plans."

"Maybe there was a plot to keep you away. You didn't need to know about your uncle's illness until afterward."

"Hamid's wife had come to my mother and said

she had found that the girl's mother was quite a gambler, and that she thought the family was too Westernized for my liking."

"Plenty of gambling in your upper classes. Why do you always refer to anything you don't like as being Western?"

"Well, if it isn't Iranian or Eastern, then it must be something else, and the only other thing there is, is Western."

"This could all be for the best. Are you sorry it isn't working out?" Sherm asked.

"Maybe I would have been happy, maybe not. Same chance you take in any marriage, no matter how it is done."

"No love at first sight then with this girl?"

"You see, our marriage contracts are on an entirely different basis than yours. Nothing so silly as affection has a part in our engagements. We think it is better if the contract is not to be the result of unthinking love. I expect to fall in love after I marry, as we get acquainted."

Ali's uncle died, which left a forty-day mourning period. Also, during this time, Ali had cooled on the girl's family and the whole idea, so it was dropped—forever.

Not long after this Ali came to call, bearing a beautiful mallard duck—already dead, but still sheathed in its feathers. He was carrying such a mountainous load we could see nothing of him but his thick black overcoat. There was the duck, hanging head down, two bouquets of flowers, one for Marlene and one for me, and big bulky sacks of wonderful fruit.

He was in a joyful mood but didn't give away the reason until we had discussed the international situation and other general subjects. Then out of the blue he pulled out his calendar and said, "Will you save a date in September along about—well—what day could you come? Take a look at my calendar and tell me which day all of you can come."

"Come to what, Ali?" I questioned.

"My wedding."

"Your wedding! Do you mean it?"

"I think so. That is, I'm 90 per cent sure. Now, what day can you come?"

"Why, this is so sudden." I was flabbergasted and stared at him in disbelief. "I don't know what to say. Have you found a girl?"

"You're right."

"Well, my, I am completely nonplused. I certainly don't want to miss this. Oh, dear, but I can't come in September! Remember—I am going to Europe with Marlene for five weeks, when she enters school in Switzerland. It will be almost the middle of October before I get back."

"Can you have it when she gets back?" Sherm inquired. "Break her heart if she had to miss the most important event in your life."

"You come back sooner. You don't have to be gone so long."

"Oh, yes I do. Lloyd was to have entered the University of Beirut, but the trouble began there, so he went on to Germany. Now he is going to go to the University of Geneva, and I want to spend some time with him, too. Getting Marlene settled and everything —I just couldn't possibly get back sooner."

"O.K.—here——" He handed me the calendar. "You pick a date."

I looked at the calendar and checked off several possibilities.

"All right, I'll have it the first day you get back. Now, you be sure to be here."

"I'll do my best, you know that— *Inshallah.*"

"Now, when are you going to give us the story on this girl, Ali?" Sherm inquired.

"Right now. That's one reason I came over. This one has blue eyes—beautiful blue eyes—and light brown hair—and, a figure——" He drew an hourglass figure in the air. "You will like her."

"Is she Iranian?" I broke in.

"Pure Iranian—with blue eyes. She is a friend of Mina and her husband. They invited me to a party soon after they were married, and this girl was there. I liked her looks. It was when I had just returned from India and seeing the Taj Mahal. I was telling the people sitting closest to me about its beauty and the love story behind it, and I noticed she was listening. Really, I was telling it to her, but she didn't know this. I didn't tell all of it on purpose, so she said she would like to hear the rest of the story, and would I tell them all of it. 'Sometime,' I said. That's the only conversation I had with her. Soon afterward Mina and Mostafa arranged another party. Then the third time I saw her was when it was her turn to have this same group at her home, so last night I was at her house."

"Where does she live?"

"Just a few blocks from you." He walked out onto the terrace and pointed at a house only three blocks away. He stood there with a dreamy look, staring in the direction of Blue Eyes' house.

"Does your mother know about this?" I had to know.

"Yes, but not that there is anything serious yet. She hasn't gone to call, but the girl's family is being investigated. Then, if Mother approves of the family, I will talk to her about calling."

"Don't you think you better wait until it is more settled before you set a date?"

"No, I don't."

He was much more determined over this girl than any other since we had known him. He either imagined himself to be infatuated, or was trying to talk himself into feeling that way.

"Does she know you are going to marry her?"

"Not yet, but I can tell she would accept me. Last night at her dinner the servants always served me first. Never took their eyes off me all evening, and when they left the room, I saw them huddled together whispering and looking toward me. This is always a sign. Let me tell you about the dinner. Never saw so much food in my life. It was the longest table." He looked around. "Almost as long as this room—with every kind of food you can imagine. Oh, it was just wonderful!" His eyes almost reflected some of the blue of Blue Eyes.

Now I wasn't sure whether he had been impressed by the girl or by the food. To an Iranian a lavish display of food gives as much prestige as a mammoth home or an expensive car.

"Ali, if her family had served a small amount of food, would you still want to marry her?"

This stopped him. He didn't answer for a minute. "If she didn't know how to be generous with her friends —yes—I guess that would have made a difference."

"The psychology of the feast really worked, didn't it?"

He had to laugh. "I guess that's right."

"You have lots of time. Why don't you wait to set the date after your mother finishes her investigation of Blue Eyes' family?"

"Look, I'm putting it down for October 6. Now you be here! For the time being, though, I am not going to tell anyone else but you two."

We knew the wedding was in the embryonic stage and could easily be tabled by either family. Since so many in each family had to be satisfied, the situation could become very complicated.

As much as we wanted to see Ali happily married, we didn't take this new romance too seriously. It brought to mind the many other times he had been on the threshold of matrimony, only to have some skeleton pop out from the prospect's background.

There was the girl from a prominent family who had had all the qualifications desired by an Iranian man, but her father was a restaurant owner. He was a member of the Majlis (House of Representatives) and accepted in the higher circles, but this could not overcome the handicap of his culinary profession. To be in the Majlis is good and very acceptable, but to be a restaurant owner, as Ali's mother said, "That is impossible! Never could you have a father-in-law who is a restaurant owner."

Then there was the girl whom the family favored, but her family made such extravagant demands in the negotiations—a trip around the world, an annual trip to Europe or the States, and enough jewelry to start a dynasty. Ali took matters into his own hands that time, and sent word back that she would get exactly one stick of wood from him—and that was all. Their return message was that they were only kidding, but Ali was not to be annoyed with any such propositions.

PERSONAL APPEARANCE

OUR GOOD FRIENDS, THE BILL MORGANS, WERE LEAV-
ing Tehran after four years of service at the University
of Tehran. We were giving them a farewell party.

I was buzzing around putting the finishing touches
on the house when Sherm telephoned.

He said, "I'm at the florist's. Say, do you have any
idea what sort of floral pieces you ordered?"

"Why, yes. Two gladioli centerpieces, one for the
dining table and one for the mantel. Why? Didn't
they make them up?"

"They sure did! I must say your ideas are extravagant. Don't you think it's a little early to enter floats
in the Pasadena Rose Parade?"

"Don't try to be funny. Just bring the flowers
home. It's getting late."

"Each one of these decorations is the size of a small
rowboat, and it will take at least four people to hoist
the one onto the mantel, then the mantel will probably
cave in. There are over 250 glads—all in mud—in
each one. Must weigh a ton. And another thing, the
robber wants seventy-five dollars for them."

"That's preposterous! I never ordered anything like
that. I showed the fellow exactly how to make them

and how many to put in. There weren't to be over a couple of dozen in each one."

"Some poor fellow is in charge who insists the manager said this is exactly what you asked for. Got your name down, even in English. Didn't you know they charge by the individual flower?"

"Look, can't you just bring four dozen of them home and I'll make my own arrangements? Tell them it isn't what I ordered, and just don't accept them."

"I'll see what I can do. Good-by." He hung up.

In a short time Sherm and our guest of honor, Bill, came staggering through the double front doors, assisted by the driver and Doran, bearing their heavy burdens. The four tugged and lugged in an undersized tin boat of gladioli. After several unsuccessful attempts, and strained muscles, they heaved it onto the dining table. Sherm had not exaggerated! He never does. The table had been expanded almost the full length of our large dining room but the enormous centerpiece nearly overshadowed it.

"Oh, no!" I wailed. "We can't have that monstrosity in here. Why didn't you do as I asked and bring just a few flowers—not this?"

"Hah! You haven't seen anything yet. Wait until you see the one for the mantel. Oh, boy! Couldn't do a thing about it. Fellow said the flowers were no good to him now that they were cut and stuck in mud, so he *made* me take them. He did make some reduction on the price, but I was still outsmarted."

I had so wanted everything to be perfect. I was

crushed. I stood, completely despondent, when Ali soundlessly entered the open door.

He startled us by gasping, "Magnificent! Those flowers are be-ut-i-ful. Oh, how the Iranians will love them. Everybody will think you are very rich to have such expensive flowers."

"Ali—you're here! Well, they will certainly be misled about the being rich part. Believe me, this is not what I ordered. Now, we don't know what to do with the thing."

"What to do with it? Just leave it alone where it is. I really mean it. It's gorgeous!" I was plucking out handfuls as he talked.

"Please—don't—don't do that, you are spoiling it." Ali raised his hand to stop me.

Sherm turned to Bill. "It's your party. Do you want it or not? Just say the word. Do you think it will detract from you too much?" He laughed.

"I'll take the chance. Leave it right here. It will give us something to remember in years to come. We will never have a floral parade float in our honor again."

I bent all efforts to doing something about the other flowerbed. It had been impossible to lift it up to the mantel, and the container would have stuck out into the room over two feet. My completed effort was no masterpiece, but I made it do with misfitting vases and too-small frogs; off and on during the party there would be an occasional thud as a few glads plunged to the floor.

Ali had come early to instruct the police we had hired to direct parking and guard the cars. We had rented a shuttle car, with driver, to bring guests to our doorstep from designated parking areas on some of the wider streets running parallel to ours.

The expected two hundred people couldn't drive down our *kutche*, with its cavernous holes and *jube* running down the middle. Only our most devoted friends ever dared to make the expedition all the way to our door. We half consciously began to measure the depth of friendship according to the number of holes each had been stuck in. The less adventurous friends always parked on a better street and walked this last block.

"Check to see if the police have come yet," I reminded Sherm.

"Just sent Mohammed down to look."

Mohammed came back to report, "Police *neist* (not)."

Ali suggested, "Have Mohammed stay down there to tell people where to park and to take the shuttle car. What we should do is make some signs, one in Farsi and one in English. All he will have to do is hand them to the drivers, then there won't be any mix-up."

Sherm and Ali quickly got two very amateurish-looking signs together and sent Mohammed on his way, but not before the first guests had arrived. Bill sneaked out the door to go get Alice. The sound of much commotion brought Sherm to the door. "Tom Burton is stuck in one of those confounded holes. Now, nobody, the shuttle—nothing can get down."

Without another word, Ali and Sherm hurried to get the four-by-fours we kept on hand for these familiar disasters and went to work.

Irene Burton huffed in. "How do you put up with this *kutche*, anyway? Just think of all the money poured into the fabulous mansions on this degenerate *kutche*. Can you imagine homes like these in the States with a crummy alley like this for a street? They wouldn't put up with it even in the worst slum area. Can't you get something done about it?"

"We've tried everything. Anyway, it's quiet. Keeps the traffic to a minimum." I was defensive.

Just then we heard a grinding squeal and anxiously looked out to see a car scraping the wall. It had gashed its left fender and made a gaping cavity in the mud and straw wall across the *kutche*.

"Whose car is that?" I cried out to Sherm, holding my breath in anticipation of the usual curses one expected from the driver's seat.

Sherm went right on shouting instructions to Tom. "Now, pull forward—turn your wheels out."

"It's a senator," I said, as I recognized the man in the back seat. "Well, it's just good enough for him. Maybe he will be moved to try to have a law passed through the Senate to have this *kutche* asphalted. We have had all the Iranians we know with political pull trying to get it done. At first we were so naïve we actually thought they were going to do something right away. Our only hope seems to be to try to persuade the Shah or Prime Minister to move onto this street, then we might get action." They had paved the next street over from ours as soon as the head of one of the Ministries completed his house there.

I sent Doran to find out from Mohammed if the

police had finally come. They had not. This was giving me the jitters, as I knew it would be catastrophic if all the cars piled up in our street. At last, they hauled Tom out of the hole and got him parked, far away— in a vacant lot.

The senator was quite upset and was giving his driver a spirited tongue-lashing.

Cars kept struggling down the *kutche,* trying to park. We had specifically asked them, in two languages on the signs, to park elsewhere, but the Iranian drivers, true to form, hadn't paid any attention.

Mohammed came back, grumbling that the guests were too important to park someplace else and go to the trouble of stepping into another car to get to our place. Furthermore, they wouldn't take directions from an ignorant gardener, and each was determined to find a spot right in front of our house.

Bill was a little late coming back with Alice, and because the shuttle car was busy shuttling, they had to walk the last block. Poor Alice's new shoes looked as if she had just walked in across the desert from Abadan. They had been white when she left home. We did the best we could with them, then turned to dusting Sherm off, so we could put up a front in the receiving line.

People began streaming in. Cars rammed into walls and each other. Finally the *kutche* was so cluttered with automobiles that the shuttle car couldn't operate, and nobody could get cars in or out.

Several other cars besides Tom's had to be fished out

of the craters. Outside, nerves were frayed, but inside everybody milled around in apparent good humor.

The Iranians were overwhelmed by the gladiolus centerpiece on the table, just as Ali had predicted. The Americans were just plain astounded.

We had rented small tables and plenty of chairs for our upper terrace. Ali stubbornly had held out for the same for the lower terrace around the pool and garden. We assumed the guests would not want to be that separated, but finally gave in.

"Iranians always head for the garden and pool. You know how we love our gardens," he had said, and he turned out to be so right.

Between the Morgans and ourselves, we recognized all the guests except two, a nice-looking Iranian girl and the man accompanying her. I thought they were friends of the Morgans; they thought the two were friends of ours.

When we discovered nobody knew them, Alice and I had a mystery on our hands. We whispered and mumbled about it between guests and wondered what one did about party crashers in the Middle East.

Whenever we were confronted with a problem we couldn't solve, we called on Ali.

"Please, Ali, come here." Alice and I both motioned to him. "See if you can find out who the party crashers are." We pointed out the girl and man.

With a queer little grin on his face he said, "Be glad to."

Alice and I took turns tramping to the terrace doors to see if Ali found the mystery couple. She raced back to report he had. It was my turn to eavesdrop. There he was, chatting affably with the two as if he were a long-lost friend. I could see the girl was pouring out her charm all over him. I was quite surprised, because it wasn't like Ali to warm up to strange women.

As the party was drawing to an end and about the time most of the guests had left, the police finally arrived. They seemed wholly unconcerned that their lateness had caused so much trouble. Sherm was glad to pay them something and tell them to go their merry way. The police left about the same time the mystery couple was leaving. Ali graciously repeated the couple's names to us as they went out the door and gave them a warm and friendly farewell.

I was bursting with curiosity. "Tell us, Ali, what did you find out?"

"They are just some people. Good family. They won't rob your house."

"Maybe not, but how strange for them to come uninvited."

"They were invited."

"No, they were not. Neither Alice nor I have ever seen them before. Bill and Sherm haven't the faintest idea who they are."

"Anyway, they were invited. They had an invitation, I know." Astonished, I opened my mouth to protest again.

"That was Blue Eyes"—he paused for effect—"and her cousin. I took one of your invitations off the pile at the university and had some mutual friends, whom you invited, give it to them. I wanted you and Sherm to see her. Well—what did you think of her? What's the verdict?"

"Oh, Ali, you rascal! Why didn't you tell us sooner so we could have had a better look?"

"Didn't want you to get your mind off the party. You would never pay any attention to the other two hundred guests if you knew Blue Eyes was in the house."

Ali came by a few days after the party. We discussed many things, but when no mention had been made of the impending wedding and after a long time I asked, "How are your wedding plans coming along?"

"They aren't. It's over—almost."

This was a bombshell because we had again been elated over another happy prospect for Ali.

"Her family. Nothing wrong with the girl, but one of her brothers is an opium addict, and, now, this is illegal. The other brother is very well known and highly respected; her father and mother are especially fine people—just that one brother isn't so good. On my own, I may have taken a chance, but my mother went to my cousin, who acts as head of the family since my father's death. You know him, the one who is such an important man in the government. He talked to me for two hours and pointed out all the reasons why I shouldn't marry Blue Eyes, the first being that it would handicap my career."

"All I can say is that it is not possible to find everyone in a family perfect. She can't help what her brother does. Why didn't you go ahead with it anyway?" Sherm remonstrated.

"You know how it is here, whatever one does in a

family reflects on the rest. Wouldn't work out with so much opposition—not a chance to succeed."

"You really did like that girl, didn't you?" I mentioned sympathetically.

"I don't know—guess so, but nothing I can do about it now. That one is finished—like all the others."

GLAD HOLIDAYS AND SAD HOLY DAYS

SPRING, LIKE SO MANY OTHER THINGS, IS BETTER IN
Iran than anywhere else—Iranians imply. Lilacs and
pink pistachio blossoms tumble over mud walls. Flower
stalls display their large pails stuffed full of narcissus
and other fragrant flowers. There is a sense of bud-
ding and blooming everywhere.

When you experienced one of these springs you knew
why Persian poets have celebrated that season in tender,
endless verse.

March 21, the first day of spring, signals the happy
holidays of the Persian New Year, *No-Ruz*, which lasts
for thirteen joyous days. This is strictly Persian, not
Moslem, and the tradition has been going on for about
five thousand years. The occasion is depicted in the
long rows of sculptured reliefs at Persepolis, showing
groups of people from every part of the great empire bringing tribute to the ruler of Persia.

We welcomed these days as enthusiastically as did
the Persians, because it is one of the very few cheerful celebrations of the year. The others are mostly
religious mourning days—and most depressing.

The first three days there is a party in every home.
Every door is thrown open, as people rush from house
to house, calling on relatives and friends.

I found many of their customs reminiscent of several of our American holidays. As we do at Christmas time, Iranians exchange cards and calls and gifts—gifts especially from the older to the young. Money, in gold or silver coins, is the preferred gift to family and close friends.

The Tuesday before the new year children masquerade in masks and veils and go from door to door of friends after dark with a large bowl and spoon, beating on the bowl and making as much racket as possible. They are invited in wherever they go and receive money, fruit, candy, and other gifts which go into the bowls. Much like our Halloween, without the tricks.

Bonfires are lit the last day of the old year and everyone, young and old, jumps over the flames as he chants a special verse. It is believed that the fire must not be breathed upon, and the dead ashes are to be scattered at a crossroads.

Then, as we do at Easter, everyone gets a new outfit—from the skin out. Eggs are gaily colored and decorated, and put on the table. These favorites of the children are symbolic of the beginning of life.

According to ancient customs, there must be on the table seven things whose names begin with the Persian letter S. There can be as many foods as the family can afford, but the basic seven must be there. The seven names are for wild rue, apples, garlic, vinegar, a paste of malt grain, greens, and sumac, all placed on a large plate. A mirror and candlesticks make up the centerpiece. Grouped around this are a copy of the Koran, a large sheet of bread, a glass of rose water, nuts, fruit, candy, chicken, and fish, and a bowl of water in which floats a green leaf or a goldfish.

The exact moment of the arrival of the vernal equinox is different each year. Our second *No-Ruz*, it appeared in Tehran at 12:30 midday. At this very second, all the household is grouped around the table to await the exciting moment which is said to be marked by the moving of the leaf or the goldfish. Nowadays, it isn't necessary to rely upon the whims of fish and leaves: the radio booms it out dramatically.

Every household is stimulated with the excitement weeks ahead, much as it must have been in our good old days when our grandmothers lovingly made fruit cakes and all the goodies for Christmas—before we could buy it all in ready-mixed packages or from the neighborhood bakery.

Fifteen days before the festival, wheat or lentils are planted in a shallow bowl in layers, one for each member of the family. This grows into a green cake, and on the thirteenth day, when everybody goes on a picnic, it is taken along and thrown away (if possible into running water) and with it go all the bad feelings and animosities of the family.

On the picnic day you see every family car loaded with many more people than it can hold, careening to the nearest patch of green grass and running water. Traffic from early morning until late at night resembles our freeways at the busy hours. Every gendarme, trainee, policeman, and police cadet is pressed into service. They are stationed every few feet on the main roads to keep things under control.

Everyone who can manage it takes a vacation at this time. There is a great exodus to the south, Shiraz and Isfahan, Abadan; and to the north to the Caspian resorts. Ali had offered to take us wherever we wanted to go. We chose the wild Turkoman country around the jungle area of Gorgon, on the Russian border. Careful plans had been made for this jaunt, but two days before we were to leave, the Iranian government forbade us to go. This was at the time of the signing of the Iran-American defense agreement, and relations with Russia were very strained; in turn, the Turkomans were restless. Even in quiet times, this is a bandit area. We appreciated the interest in our welfare, and although disappointed, made alternate plans.

Ali always came up with something. "Let's go to Shiraz. We know we have a place to stay, and you can be in the heart of a real *No-Ruz* celebration."

We agreed to this; then the day before we were to leave, Sherm found himself sitting on Pahlavi in a tired, clunked-out automobile. He finally got towed to the garage, where the car was diagnosed as needing new rings and bearings. This repair job would take several days. We had planned to take our car this time, but Ali said it presented no problem as we would take his car. Then Ali lent his car to a friend, who landed in a *jube,* and this put his car in the garage. Ali took a taxi to our home to relay the bad news.

"Now don't worry, we are going to go. I am not

going to have you disappointed. Somehow we will go."
He never gave up on anything.

Somehow we did go. Later that same day Ali ginger-
ly stepped into our house and motioned us outside.
There he proudly displayed a new Volkswagen he had
just bought. "O.K., we can take our trip. How do
you like it? Is it all right?"

"Why, it's great, but whose is it?" Sherm asked.

"It's yours. For the *No-Ruz* season—it is yours. Do
anything you want with it."

"But I don't understand. Somebody must have paid
for it."

"Oh, I bought it, but I'm lending it to you for the
time being."

"That's just like you, Ali," Sherm said accurately.
"What will you do when you get your car out of the
garage? You can't drive two cars at once."

"I'll face that when the time comes. Anyway, now
we have a car."

Ali's devoted little mother was up early to wish us
well. She was staying in town with her many relatives because she was not well, but it would be one of
the few times Ali had been separated from her during
No-Ruz. After calling for us, Ali stopped by his home
again to tell her good-by. She stood in the open doorway with a velvet-bound copy of the Koran in her
upraised hand. Ali touched it lightly with both palms,
bent his head and kissed it. His mother lifted the book
above his head and murmured a silent prayer. She
offered the same blessing for all of us. Ali respectfully
kissed her hand, then squeezed into the car. The first

thing he did was to make sure his own tiny Koran was fastened securely to the steering wheel for our protection.

Our original three travelers had increased to five. Iranians prefer a crowd, so we were not surprised when two of Ali's male cousins piled into the car the last minute. Although the Volks was just barely large enough for Sherm, Ali, and me, we realized we were lucky that out of deference to our comfort he had invited only two cousins.

It seemed the whole of Iran was snaking its way to Shiraz. We planned to make it to Isfahan the first night, where we could stay with other Ali cousins.

We had taken along only water and some crackers; we had so little room, and besides, we assumed there would be an occasional teahouse or some place we could obtain food. However, we had not fully reckoned with Ramazan, the religious month of fasting, when restaurants are closed during the daytime. As luck would have it, this year Ramazan fell at the same time as No-Ruz. It happens every thirty-six years, and this was the year! What confusion, with mourning days superimposed upon a happy holiday! The people didn't know whether to be glad or sad. The more devout Moslems had picked Ramazan, and chose to fast and pray, while the less devout Persians chose No-Ruz.

Ramazan is observed through the entire Moslem world. It is a month taken from the Arabic Lunar Calendar. The lunar year is ten days shorter than the calendar (now used in Iran since 1925). Thus the two occasions coincide every thirty-six years.

It was during Ramazan that Mohammed received the Koran from heaven. It is said, "During Ramazan the gates of paradise are open, the gates of hell shut, and the devil in chains." Moslems believe, "He who fasts has two delights, breaking his fast and meeting the Lord."

In Iran all social functions are banned, movie theaters, cafes, and other public places are closed during the deep mourning days of Ramazan; good Moslems abstain from food, drink, tobacco, and physical pleasure from sunup to sundown. Exempted from fasting are soldiers on duty, travelers, sick people, pregnant women, and children. For the sick the abstentions can be made up at a later time.

When a white thread may be distinguished from a black one, then another day's fast begins. The hours of sunrise and sunset change slightly each day. In cities, a cannon shot announces the hour to break the fast while in the villages the muezzin sings out the call to prayer. Our servants relied on Radio Tehran.

The Prophet's idea was to have the people eat only twice a day and give the rest of the food to the poor. Nowadays, a celebration begins at sundown. The feasting begins by saying, "In the name of Allah, bless the food!" It is a happy, merry time, with visiting back and forth among families. At the end of the thirty days there is a great three-day feast.

When the great mullah at Qum announced that by the moon Ramazan was over, I was every bit as elated as our servants, Mohammed and Doran. They had never wavered from the fast. The first three days were their worst; after that, they claimed their systems became accustomed to it, and they didn't mind it so much. A long, dismal period, nevertheless.

That should have been an example to me—these people who could go without food — but it wasn't. Here I was, just a little late for lunch, since we had breakfast so early, and I was famished. I should have had my mind on *No-Ruz* as this was *the* day, but I had it on *food*.

I ate more than my share of the crackers; that kept me from being too obnoxious for a while longer. As we putted along, Ali kept looking at his watch. I thought he was trying to figure out how long it would take us to reach the next village—and food. But without any comment, he suddenly drove to the side of the road, stopped the car dead, and without explanation, hopped out. He ran to the desert stretch along the road and began picking up bits of brush and dry wood. Then he motioned emphatically for his two cousins to come and help. Sherm and I just sat there watching the three run up and down, piling up brushwood directly in the path of our car, making a barricade all the way across the road. Two cars ran through the bushes, so Ali planted himself in the middle and began flagging down cars, at the same time shouting to them something in Persian.

"This is certainly strange. So unlike Ali. Do you think I better get out and see what it the matter with him?" Sherm asked me.

"I guess we still don't know Persians. Or maybe the desert sun's getting him. What in the world?"

Just then Ali set fire to the bushes with his cigarette lighter. We scrambled out of the car, just in case it went up with the flames.

Ali scurried over to us and pointed to the time on his watch. "It's now—exactly—12:19—the very moment of the new year here." He kissed Sherm on the cheeks and swung him around in a circle, shook hands with me, and went on to his cousins.

The cars were now lined up for at least a quarter of a mile. Ali was racing from one to another, proclaiming the new year. Everyone was out of the cars by this time. Someone down the line had produced a portable phonograph and after a vigorous windup began playing some modern Persian dance tunes.

At least a hundred people were congregated along the road. All walks of life were represented, which made it an exceptional social gathering for this culture. Men were kissing one another, shouting, singing, and dancing. People were jumping over the burning bushes. Three men were carrying gallon jugs of wine, passing them to all and urging a toast to the new year. The wine drinkers were definitely not good Moslems.

An ancient horse-drawn wagon came along from the opposite direction with an old workman at the reins. Ali climbed up beside him, kissed him all over his dirty face, put a large-size rial note under his round hat, then jumped down. Then he pulled the man out of the wagon, took off his beanie hat, and began passing it through the crowd.

Following the lead, everyone put money in the hat, and when it was overflowing, Ali helped the old man back into his wagon. The poor old fellow was dumfounded. We crowded around his wagon along with others, and when we moved closer we could see the tears blurring his vision. He was bowing and talking animatedly. Ali translated to us, "He says he has never seen so much money in all his life. He is so excited he doesn't know what to do. He is driving that boogy for someone else. Doesn't own a thing in the world, evidently."

"You mean 'buggy,' only he isn't driving a buggy— it's a wagon."

Ali laughed and laughed at his own mispronunciation. "Anyway, boogy, buggy, or wagon, now he is happy." With that Ali dashed up and down handing out silver coins until he had emptied his pockets of all he had—fifty of them. Then he came back to us, gave a gold coin to me and one to Sherm, and said, "Hope you get lots of gold this year." Then he motioned to us, "Come on—you dance. See, everybody is dancing now."

We caught their exuberance. This was the first time we had seen Iranians evidencing much outward happiness. We did our own improvisations, up and down in the dusty highway, like the rest of them. The people were delighted that foreigners would join in and began standing around us, clapping their hands.

Dusty and grimy, and happy, we continued on our way. In the excitement, I had forgotten my hunger. However, at the very next village, Ali canvassed the mud huts, and although everyone seemed to be fasting, he was able to get some of yesterday's *pillo* for us.

After it was reheated it almost tasted good. Ali was as ravenous as I. He was not observing the fast. When we asked him why not, his answer was, "you see, travelers are exempt, and I am only traveling through this life—so——"

"Your mother is a good Moslem; is she fasting?" Sherm inquired.

"No, because she is in poor health. That excuses her. If she were well she would be fasting. The other day she gave a mullah one hundred dollars to fast for my dead father, because sometime in his life he missed a few fasts. She feels this will help him wherever he is."

"Do you think it will?" I asked dubiously.

"Well, do I look crazy? She will never know whether the mullah fasted for her, and I am not one who believes one person can save another, anyway. The point is that it makes her feel better so maybe it's worth the one hundred dollars—that is the main thing."

Isfahan and Ali's cousin Kareem's home looked mighty good to us late that evening. Although we were unexpected guests, a delicious dinner was quickly ready for us, and we spent a wonderful night with them.

After many accidents and delays we got to Shiraz the next night. Over 50,000 other visitors had preceded us, and people were sleeping on the streets and all over the place. Thank goodness, this would not be our lot, as we had a place to stay.

Because our plans had been changed, Ali's brother, the colonel, had not anticipated us and had gone to the family villages.

We had been guests twice before in this house; everything was familiar and we felt very much at home. At night our regular dormitory arrangements were set up—half the rooms went to the women, the other half to the men.

The first three days we were treated as part of the family and joined in the frenzied visits, going from house to house all day long, visiting, drinking tea, and eating the miniature cookies and sweets made especially for *No-Ruz*. This was permissible because we were travelers and Christians.

The fourth morning Ali and two of his gentleman friends did not appear for breakfast. Just as we finished, the three came dragging in, looking like cats who had just swallowed canaries, and rather weary— as if they had been on some all-night escapade.

"Where have you been?" someone asked.

The three looked sheepish and passed it off with a wisecrack in Farsi. At least, I assumed that is what it was, as everyone laughed and no more questions were asked.

Later in the day I cornered Ali. "Say, where did you find a place to go around here that was interesting enough to keep you up all night?"

He gave me that self-conscious grin. "Wouldn't you like to know?"

"Yes, I really would. How about taking us next time, wherever you went. We don't want to miss anything, you know."

"All right, I will, but somehow I'm not sure you would enjoy it. I think this is one time you would have to be a born Iranian, not an adopted one, to comprehend this sort of thing. We Iranians have lots of problems, we worry a lot but keep it deep inside until sometime we just have to let it out. Well, this was one of those times. The two fellows who went with me wanted to talk to a dervish. You know, he is a holy man."

"I thought a dervish was something like a Christian monk. They don't believe in material things, own nothing, and live by their wits—is that right?"

"There are a lot of fakes who just live off the people, but some are deeply religious. A genuine dervish sort of renounces the world; he is an ascetic who lives in the world but still out of it—if you know what I mean. Some are great philosophers. They lead a more wandering life here in Iran than in most countries. Anyway, the one we went to see is a famous one about whom everyone knows. He lives on a hill outside of town— alone—away from everything. He is supposed to be a very good and sincere man. The fellows wanted me to take them to see him, so I did. They drank wine and poured out their suffering souls to him for two hours. They wept and released all their—what you call it—ah—buried emotions, and now they feel better. I didn't feel like joining in this time, I just waited for them. They came and got me out of bed at three o'clock this morning."

"Very interesting. I think it's beneficial that your people, or any people for that matter, can find harmless ways to release these feelings. When the people show their emotions unabashed in your mosques, shrines, and cemeteries, it seems it's good emotional therapy."

"You know, I did a similar thing in India not long ago. One moonlight night I was sitting with another man at the foot of the Taj Mahal. The man was overcome at the beauty of it all, so he began to sob and cry his heart out. Then I began to reflect on the beautiful love story behind it, and before I knew what was happening I went to pieces and did the same thing. It was like a dream. I felt as if I were in another world and was another person. Afterward, I couldn't even remember how long I sat there. I'll never, never in my life forget that experience."

Our Iranian New Year holiday week had been very social and entertaining, and now that it had drawn to a close, we were going on to a village where the men in our party planned to hunt. As we were packing, Ali received a telephone call from the colonel. During the conversation Ali's face clouded. He hung up the receiver without saying a word. His body sagged in dejection as he took out a cigarette, lit it, and began slowly to puff on it. After a few tense minutes he broke the silence.

"They are having a terrible time in the villages— just awful. The locusts are swarming in from Saudi Arabia by the millions—they are making such heavy clouds the people can't even see the sun. They are demolishing every crop in southern Fars. Locusts are bad enough, but there are even grasshoppers—all at the same time." He gave a hopeless gesture. "Over 1,500 men in our village alone are battling them, but they can't get anywhere. Locusts devour everything they touch, fallen cattle, even a human if he can't get up. I saw them down there when I was a boy. The colonel says it's so dreadful you can't even imagine!"

"That's horrible, Ali. Wish there was something could be done. Nothing but spray from planes will do any good. Is the government aware of the situation?" Sherm inquired.

"Yes, they are trying to do something, but it will take a lot more planes than we have. When you farm land there is always some disaster. Last year the *Qanat* went out (a *qanat* is an underground channel, a method of irrigation unique in Iran). This year it's the locusts. I wanted to go down and help, but my brother says what can I do when 1,500 men can't do anything."

"If the crops are destroyed how will the villagers eat during the winter?" Sherm continued.

"That's the problem. We will have to do as we did last year—help feed them and keep them alive. That will mean three thousand to feed again this year. Oh, boy, there are two sides to this business of owning villages."

"Nobody knows better than we do since we own farmland ourselves. If it isn't the hail, it's the grass-hoppers, the drouth, frost, floods, rust, or something," Sherm said.

"As long as I can't help—let's go on to the village and hunt," said Ali.

We left the main road out of Shiraz and took off on make-it-yourself roads. It was nothing but desert, no car tracks, no cow trails—just desert. We zigzagged over old river beds, maneuvered around rock piles, up sides of hills so steep that the four men had to push while I steered the car.

Our journey ended in a small village that clung precariously to the side of the mountain. A mud wall surrounded the outside; the houses were made of mud and straw, with flat roofs of the same materials. The houses were built in a square with small yards or compounds inside. When there was room, and the villager was fairly well off, there were a few trees or grapevines and a small pool of water. If there was no pool, there was a stream running through the compound, where the villager washes his feet, his dishes, or empties his garbage to float on to the next compound.

The huts were about five feet above the level of the ground to keep the rooms dry from excess rain, and by that design the goats, chickens, and cows are less likely to wander in and out.

Ali charmed the headman into allowing us to stay in his home. His was the largest in the village, not large according to our standards, nor were we to enjoy the comforts of home.

Our sleeping quarters lay under the stars: the brick floor of the compound, a Persian rug, a cotton pad, and some cotton comforters (reading from the bottom up). After sundown, the Moslems who were fasting could eat, and the headman joined us. Our dinner consisted of boiled eggs, tea, flat Iranian bread, and yoghurt. Breakfast was identical, with the addition of some canned juice we'd brought along.

Like most villages, this one was owned by an absentee landlord. Eighty per cent of the population of

Iran live in these small villages, and their average per capita income is less than one hundred dollars a year.

Some of them had not seen a car before. I thought they would have most of the paint off and the upholstery worn from feeling it. I was to be left behind to make room for some villager who would act as a guide on the hunt. There was a mad scramble to see who would have the honor of accompanying the men, as much for the adventure of riding in the car as for the money.

My means of communication with the villagers was limited, so I spent most of my time watching them go about their daily tasks. At the edge of a stream of water running through this village, several women spent much of their time squatting, washing clothes and gossiping. Some used sand in lieu of soap. I kept my *chador* on, but, nevertheless, I was an oddity and, one by one during the day the women paraded by and gaped at me. For our protection, Ali had told them we had escaped from Baghdad during the revolution there.

Sometimes these village people are fanatical and will not allow a non-Moslem to be around them, eat near them, or touch anything in their homes. We are considered unclean.

They were all fasting. There wasn't much left for me to do but join them—much against my will, believe me! Now and then I would sneak a cracker and swallow it in one gulp when no one was looking.

Sitting all day long and doing nothing was downright strenuous. It made me realize what a monotonous life the two-headed men, the fat lady, the giant, and

Persian Village

other freaks lead in the side show of a circus. I tried
to read a book I'd brought along, but there was so
much mute company staring at me it was not con-
ducive to concentration. The onlookers couldn't even
read Farsi, so no chance they would discover my book
was in English instead of Arabic. They had probably
never heard of the English language, or of America.

It was a happy reunion when my traveling companions returned safely that night.

Sherm came marching in carrying an ibex on his
back, with the legs draped over his shoulders, and a
smile on his face that would have lit up Times Square.
I knew what this meant to him, as he had longed to
bag an ibex. Hunting for them is hazardous, and they
are very smart and harder to shoot than deer.

They all began to talk at once. Sherm finally got
the floor, "Boy, oh boy, was it ever rugged. All the
villagers wear those woven cotton shoes with pieces
of tire tread on the bottoms, and that's pretty smart
because it isn't as hard for them to cling to the rocks.
But you should have seen me with my leather soles.
I would take one step forward and slip back three.
More times than I can count I just caught myself as
my gun and I were about to take off on a header down
the mountainside. Almost didn't get back—alive."

"That's right, he had too many close calls," Ali added.

"I had plenty of time to think about just that all
day," I said. "I could have worked up a good case of
hysteria thinking what would happen to me if you
never got back. I probably would have had to spend
the rest of my life here." I wouldn't make a very

good second, or even third or fourth wife for any of these old codgers. I'm glad you're back."

Everyone crowded 'round to admire the ibex. It is a species of mountain goat, about the size of a small deer and considered a great delicacy. Never have I eaten more tender and delicious meat—than ibex meat.

The next day we moved on to another village where the partridge were supposed to be thicker than the fleas in the village we'd just left.

Here Ali found a house where we would have to share a room with only an old woman and her husband. It was late at night when we arrived, so when the headman awakened the couple, it was quite a shock to them, especially to see the two strange foreigners. The old lady was so flustered with it all that, as she came forward to greet us, she fell headlong into the compound pool. Sherm sprinted to her and pulled her out, *chador* and all. She was a good sport about it, and, although dripping wet, she went about trying to scrape up some food for us with her only two teeth chattering audibly against her upper gums.

"You know something, Sherm?" Ali was confidential. "You are the only man besides that old woman's husband who has ever touched her hand. She is a devout Moslem." He laughed. "I'll bet she would like to do it all over again just to have a big handsome, blue-eyed man touch her hand once more."

This gave me an idea. For a split second I wondered if I should drop into the pool myself to get a little attention for a change and just for a few minutes get their minds off ibex and partridge. But I thought better of it; no doubt I would drown, or they would just tell me to swim out. And the green, slimy water was most uninviting, and it must have been freezing cold.

We were guided into the room we would share with the elderly couple. It was small, and a *korsi* took up the center, so when all seven of us crowded in, there wasn't much room left around the edges.

A *korsi* will never replace central heating, but nothing could have given more welcome warmth that chilly night than that primitive but effective heating arrangement.

Actually, the *korsi* is a giant community bed with a common warming pad. I had never shared such cozy sleeping arrangements with so many people before. The experience was well worth remembering.

The *korsi* was made of unpainted, rough boards, about six feet by six feet, placed on top of short legs which stood about as high as a low, modern coffee table. Underneath was a perforated pail of hot charcoal. Tossed over the top of the whole thing were several well-worn quilts. The idea is to put your feet in toward the *korsi*, pull the quilts over you, stretch out, and put your head on the bags of wool which serve for pillows.

Thus disposed, we all looked like so many spokes in a wheel.

I could see Sherm was envious of me because I had brought along my own pillow (against all protests), and on the entire trip it turned out to be very smart of me.

Ali brought in his two lightweight, clean tribal rugs,

one of which he handed to me to put next to my body before the community quilts went on.

I snuggled over toward Sherm as much as I dared in this Moslem atmosphere. I was so fascinated with the idea of sleeping on a mud floor, in a tiny room with no windows, only a piece of cloth for a door, and six companions in far-off Persia that I was the last one to fall asleep.

It was still dark when Ali and Sherm rolled out from under the *korsi*. This roused the old woman, who got up, left, and returned with an *aftabeh* (Persian water pitcher) full of water from the stream. She poured the water over their hands for a quick wash. They filled their pockets with shotgun shells, added a few pomegranates and pieces of *sanyak* (bread) to their knapsacks, picked up their shotguns, and told me I'd better get moving, as they were ready to go.

The two cousins piled out, went through the same procedure, and were ready in no time at all. I got the same treatment and considered myself ready, in spite of aching to brush my teeth and get out of all my rumpled clothes into something that hadn't been slept in.

It had been decided, the night before, that I would go with them for partridge; the terrain would not be as dangerous as for ibex. I felt sure that any discomfort I would have following them would not be as monotonous as spending the day in that dark room, with no one to talk to and nothing to do but try to keep my *chador* on—which was a job for me—and be stared at all day long.

I was concerned about the adequacy of my walk-

Under a Korsi

ing shoes for the rock and shale of the mountainsides, but Sherm assured me anything that could make it down our *kutche* would do on most mountain passes. Anyway, they promised that I could take the low places, and they would climb the ridges.

The men started off at a fast pace, and with my shorter legs I had a hard time keeping even close to them. We headed for a grove of walnut trees up the valley where we could see where a small stream of water must originate. As we approached, Ali signaled for everybody to walk quietly, and he carried his gun in readiness. This spot was one where partridge usually came for water and food before disappearing onto the high ridges during the day.

As usual, Ali had figured correctly, because within a few minutes, both he and Sherm were blasting away at a covey of partridge as they flew off in twenty different directions.

Ali ran at top speed off into the bushes, and Sherm dashed in another direction as soon as the shooting ceased. I could hear them thrashing around, then in a few minutes both emerged into the clearing, Ali holding up three birds, and Sherm one.

"I knocked down three," Sherm said, "but in those bushes you can't tell where they are hiding. Just my luck to lose those, and I may never get another shot at a partridge all day."

"Now that you have got one," Ali philosophized, "you will have the strength to walk for miles until you get dozens more. See what nice fat ones these are. Plenty of food and water around here to make them

fat. Wait until you have these cooked with raisin *pillo*.
It's wonderful! O.K. Where is your knife?"

"Right here in my pocket. Why?"

"We must cut the jugular vein of the birds immediately."

"Never heard of that. I've shot pheasants, ducks,
prairie chickens, and all kinds of birds for years, but
we have never done anything like that to them. What's
the idea?"

"Part of our religion. We believe that if the blood
is left in an animal after it is killed, it will spoil the
flesh. There may be some disease in the blood, and
we must get rid of it at once. Here, let me have your
knife and I'll show you what we do."

It was all I could do to show an interest in the birds,
because I can't stand to look at dead birds, especially
such beautiful ones, and I think hunters are cruel anyway to kill them; and secondly, to watch anything
bleeding simply sickens me. I turned my head, but
then I was curious to see what Ali was going to do,
so I peeked again. He held the partridge by the head
with one hand, and sawed through the under part of
the bird's neck with the other. The blood spurted all
over Sherm's shirt; whereupon Ali held the partridge
by the feet so the blood would drip down onto the
ground. Whereupon, I almost fainted.

"Here, you hold this one while I let the blood out
of my three." Ali handed it to Sherm. "Then we better
hurry on up to that next bunch of trees and see if we
can scare up some more." Ali proceeded with the oper-

ation while I cringed with each slash of the knife and kept my head well turned.

About noon, in spite of fair luck and some pomegranate juice, I was ready to call it a day. Sherm could see I was tired, so he suggested that he and I start back down the valley and Ali could cut on over the hill with his cousins if he wished, meeting us back in the village. I caught Ali's look of disgust—to him, women had no place on a hunting trip anyway, and he was visualizing how many more birds he and Sherm would have gotten if I had stayed home.

However, as accommodating as usual, Ali agreed, and he and his cousins took off up the side of the mountain as Sherm and I plodded on back down the valley.

When we drove into Tehran after our holiday, it looked unbelievably modern and civilized.

GLITTER AND GOLD

FROM A TRAIN WINDOW, EN ROUTE TO ABADAN, I SAW
the gleaming, gold-domed, sacred shrine at Qum. Since
then, I had longed to return to that holy city before
I left Iran. Time was running out, and soon we would
be leaving.

Qum is the second most sacred city of Iran, after
Meshed. It is at Qum that the great Mullah, who is
to the Shi'a Moslems what the Pope is to the Catholics,
reigns supreme. Here, too, are the principal Shi'a Moslem schools for training mullahs. The presence in the
city of any non-Moslem is frowned upon by devout
followers.

The glory of Qum is the gold-domed tomb of Fatima,
sister of the eighth Imam and a revered saint. Thousands of pilgrims have visited the tomb yearly for
centuries. It is said that twelve kings and four hundred princes and saints are buried in this shrine. Shah
Abbas, one of the greats, is among these. Legend re-
lates that Fatima came to live in Qum after fleeing
from persecutions in Baghdad, and was buried here in
A.D. 816.

The courtyard of the shrine is a unique sanctuary
(*bast*). All outlaws who succeed in reaching it are

protected. Old women, who thus store up rewards in heaven, bring them food.

Whenever I told my desire to visit this shrine to Iranian friends, shocked silence followed; then they would launch into a harangue about the fanaticism of the pilgrims there, and the many sinister things which could happen to me, the least of which would be death by beating.

"One of the things I want more than anything to see while I am here is the shrine of Qum," I had casually said to Maryam Niami.

"No, I don't think you better try. They have been known to beat foreigners to death there."

"But I would wear a *chador* and no one would know. Besides, I could well be a Moslem. How would they know what my religion is?"

"But you are foreign. They would know that. You know I am not a very good Moslem and I don't like all these shrines and things too much, but I do know how fanatical those people can be."

Several examples of the killing of non-Moslems at lesser shrines and in mosques were cited, and I knew them to be true, for it had even happened to one of our American consulate members in Shiraz.

One day I said to Ali, "Please, won't you take me to visit Fatima's shrine at Qum? You know I have great sympathy and understanding for your religion, and I only want to see for myself what one of your sacred tombs is like. It will help me to get a still better insight into your faith. Of course, I wouldn't want to go if it would be offensive, but no one has given

me a genuine reason as to what harm I could possibly
be doing. Is there anything in your religion against it?"

There was a long, unbroken silence, then Ali cleared
his throat and thoughtfully replied, "There is nothing
in the Koran which says a non-Moslem can't look. I
don't know of anything written or spoken against such
things by Mohammed. The problem is that in our
religion, as in all of them, we have these crazy fanatics
who take it upon themselves to make their own laws.
They are still fighting the old religious wars. I hate
fanatics. They hurt our religion. They are far away
from the Koran and the true teachings of the Prophet."

Ali paused. "Maybe it would be better if you went
to a mosque. It would still be a problem, but would
that satisfy you?"

"As long as there is nothing in your religion against
my going to the shrine, I truly would love to see it.
I have heard it is so beautiful. It must be, for pilgrims to sacrifice as they do to come from all over
to worship there. The sanctuary for criminals, too,
intrigues me very much."

"You could cover up with a *chador* and perhaps
nobody would be able to figure out you are foreign,
but if Sherm wants to go, I will have to say right
now that we couldn't take the risk with him. He is
too big, too light—and he can't hide behind a *chador*."

"He isn't interested anyway." I turned to Sherm.
"Are you, dear?"

"No. I'll ride down with you, but not go all the
way into the city."

Before Ali could change his mind I pinned him

down to a day. We finally decided on the day after
the rites of Ali's (the Imam's) death.

"This is a bad day to go because there will be lots
of people weeping and crying and making lots of racket,
but since it is the only one Sherm and I both have
off at the same time, we better go. May as well get
it over with," said Ali.

The plan was for Sherm and the car to wait for us
on the outskirts of the city while we took a taxi into
town. "Better see if you can disguise him a little bit,
because we don't want him to be conspicuous while
just sitting there alone," Ali had advised.

I tried all kinds and shapes out of our collection of
tribal gear on him but gave up. It was impossible to
conceal his foreignness. He then got his own getup
together, a Daniel Boone type of fur-lined hat (this
made him somewhat resemble a Russian Cossack), a
two-day beard, and a vague mustache slightly dark-
ened with my eyebrow pencil. As I look back I wonder how he escaped with his life. He looked more like
an American tramp than anything else and Sherm
would have been much less noticeable playing himself.

Ali felt the need of reinforcements. Although we
will never know how many relatives turned him down,
he finally persuaded his cousin, Hossein, to go with
us. Afterward we learned that Hossein had thought
we'd just be driving around the shrine—not actually
trying to enter.

The four of us set out on the indescribably rough,
roller-coaster roads to Qum, rattling along, diving from

rut to rut. The shock absorbers gave way the first five miles out and we had a hundred yet to go.

"Even if I should look slightly suspect," I said as we jogged on, "there is nothing to worry about because, Ali, no one would guess that a good Moslem face like yours would walk with an infidel to a sacred shrine. You know, to me and Sherm you are Mr. Iran. You are exactly as we visualized a Persian to be. Black eyes, gallant, mysterious. Besides, you have been to Mecca, Kerbela, and all the sacred places. Surely they would never question an old hadji, a man who has taken the pilgrimage to Mecca, and especially a direct descendant of Mohammed."

"Yes, I traveled to Mecca and went through fifteen days of the required religious procedure, but it was not at the pilgrimage time of year, so I am only half a hadji."

"Heavens, will they quibble over that?"

"They don't ask questions—they just act. They are like sheep. Someone yells *ferangi* (foreigner) and the hundreds of them attack. That's all."

Nobody talked for quite a while, then Ali ordered, "Repeat this after me," and went into what I thought was Persian. He was always trying to teach us new words and sayings. I repeated the first few words, but not to his satisfaction. After several attempts he accepted it, then made me go over and over it until I could say it myself.

After he had finished with me, I said, "O.K., now, what did I say? What were all those words? I got 'Allah,' but I can't make sense out of it."

"You have just become a Moslem," he said, and he didn't smile.

"Ah, you're kidding! It would take a mullah to do that."

"Yes, the accepted way nowadays is to say it before a mullah. However, you can say those words to anybody, anywhere, or even just to yourself, and become a Moslem—if you believe them."

"What is the translation?"

"You said, in Arabic—the Koran is in Arabic, the language of our religion—'I testify there is no Allah but one Allah, I testify that Mohammed is the prophet of Allah.' That's all there is to it."

"All right, now that I'm a Moslem, how do I get out of being one?" I laughed.

By his expression I realized this wasn't a joke to Ali. "That's your protection. I know what you said —so to me you are a Moslem, and I can swear it if anyone should ask. I tried to teach you the Arabic words, so if there is a problem you could say them. You didn't understand what you were saying, so as far as you are concerned you haven't changed your religion—but, anyway, I feel better."

He pulled out a small Koran from his breast pocket, kissed it, and returned it to its place.

Cousin Hossein spoke very little English, but at the halfway point, he said, "You fix——." He pointed to my *chador*.

I swung it around, slapping everyone in the face in so doing. I couldn't seem to get the middle on top of my head, but, as least, I was haphazardly covered.

"Hossein says you must wear it now all the rest of the way. These crowds of people going by in buses and taxis may recognize us."

Ali watched me fuss and fiddle, trying to get it to cover my hair. "Let's see how you look with just your eyes showing." I tried to comply.

"No, it won't do with your nose sticking out—it doesn't look Persian."

I could cover my nose and one eye but couldn't let both my eyes show without baring my nose.

"Cover all—everything but one eye."

Ali turned to Hossein. "Do you think she will do like this?"

Hossein answered him in Persian. Ali interpreted, "He's getting afraid. He thinks maybe the *chador* will slip off your head, then no telling what would happen to all of us. Get a good grip on it."

I gripped, I adjusted and readjusted, but wisps of hair kept popping out, then my whole face would fall out.

"Your lipstick—get that off—and the—what you call it—face paint."

"I'll have my mouth covered," I said, but just the same I energetically rubbed away at the lipstick.

They let me out of the car between the passing of two heavily loaded buses, and told me to get the *chador* on straight. One side was dragging on the ground while the other came only to my waist. I certainly hadn't got the center where it should be. There is an art to wearing a *chador*, and it takes practice. As yet I did not have the flare for it.

I had pulled on the heavy black stockings I had purchased for the occasion and I felt the leg masquerade
was quite faultless. "Your shoes. They will never do.
Too bright—white and black. Persian women pilgrims
won't be wearing shoes like that. Put those others back
on—those— those brown ones," Ali demanded.

"O.K., but it takes forever to get them on and off."

"Then they will never do. Just keep those white
ones on, but remember when you take them off and
put them on, you have to do it in such a way that
you won't lose your *chador*, and try not to be clumsy."

I leaned down to try it out and, sure enough, the
chador slid off.

"Are you still determined to go to the shrine?" Ali
seemed to be weakening.

"Please don't worry. This won't happen in the final
performance. You know, we always say that everything goes wrong at dress rehearsals." I laughed nervously.

"This isn't funny; it's very serious," Ali remonstrated.

"I know it is. I swear that I'll get a death grip on
this *chador*, so don't be apprehensive." I got back into
the car.

The closer we got to the city the more voluble Hossein became.

"He doesn't really think it is a good idea to try to
go inside. He says why don't we drive around it, then
have a picnic someplace?" Ali was interpreting for
his cousin. "You see it takes a long time to learn to
wear a *chador* without being—what you call it—like

a beginner—awkward." Now I was afraid Hossein was going to back out.

As we came to the outskirts of Qum, Ali signaled. "Stop here, Sherm. This is a good place. Now, just remember these pilgrims are rabid. For instance, the fanatics think if a Moslem has changed to another religion that he should be killed. You see how crazy they think. Keep your *chador* on—all over you—and don't show any part of your dress or your face, just that one eye."

The three of us told Sherm good-by and started walking toward town and a taxi.

"Sherm, always remember this was her idea, not mine," Ali called back and, as he said this, whisked off his tie and stuffed it into his pocket.

"Why did you do that?" I asked.

"Several reasons. To show respect we loosen our collars and take off our ties. For funerals or whenever we want to be very respectful—like today. Also, with a tie on I might be taken for a foreigner. Another thing, some people think a tie and collar look like the sign of a cross."

I fretted inside my covering. "I am suffocating in here."

"Rather have you smother to death than be beaten to death. Just be glad you can hide in that thing. Be careful—no false moves——" Ali was adamant.

A taxi stopped for us. Ali became strictly Persian and left me on my own. I got wound up in the door handle trying to turn it with my hand still inside the *chador*. The men got in the other side and I slammed the door on my *chador,* but rather than create a disturbance I just let the end of it whip outside in the breeze, all the way.

The shining golden dome had been visible miles away, and now, as we drove closer, we could see a battery of blue-tiled minarets coming into full view, a bold, impressive contrast to the vast desert expanse.

We stepped out at the entrance of the courtyard. Ali and Hossein did not give me one flicker of recognition, but walked solemnly in, looking straight ahead. I kept my head and eyes downcast as instructed and well remembered Ali's admonition, "Whatever you do, don't look at any men."

I fastened my eyes on my shoes. They seemed to grow whiter and whiter and more glaring with every step. There were many people milling about the tremendous courtyard.

Glancing up, I saw an oblong pool where people were washing their arms and feet in preparation for entering the mosque which adjoined the shrine. You are not allowed to enter the mosque unless you have performed these ablutions. A few surreptitious side glances revealed many men in rags. I wondered if they were the refugee criminals.

It was a long walk to the tomb and seemed, under the strain, much farther.

I rolled my eye up in its socket as far as I dared, without rolling it all the way out, and glimpsed the sparkling, opulent front of faceted mirrors.

Lowering my eyes, I saw Ali's feet coming out of his shoes, so I knew we had reached the check-stand entrance. I had barely stepped out of mine when Hossein brushed them up with his in one rapid swoop, and handed them all together to the checkman. At that moment the realization gripped me that my shoes had an American brand label in them. A worried side glance, however, showed me that the three pairs of shoes had been tossed together into slots. With so many pilgrims swarming around, they evidently had no time for detective work on footwear.

Ali walked ahead. I followed with Hossein close behind me. My head was bowed as low as possible. Many heads were bowed in prayer along the sides of the wall. We stepped in, and the brilliance of the scene (even looking with only one eye) surpassed all my expectations. Such radiance, glitter, mirror work, and gilt!

A man approached us immediately and spoke to me —I thought. My heart pounded—I knew I couldn't answer him. I had a violent urge to go—get out. Ali answered him. I should have known, a man in such a sacred place would not speak to a woman.

I continued to follow Ali's footsteps as he backed against a wall, Hossein stood riveted where he entered. The man began to chant prayers for us. As he droned on I took advantage of the respite to squint around.

Directly in front of us, within touching distance, was the tomb of Fatima. The black covering of what seemed to be a casket was inside a silver cage crisscrossed with ornate bars. Men and women were clinging to the sides of it, clawing through the bars, kissing, caressing it, praying, and weeping. The continual stream of humanity circled round and round, repeating

At Fatima's Shrine

all these emotions again and again. Little children imitated their mothers and tried to push their heads through the bars while they wept bitterly. It seemed I was witnessing the greatest tragedy of the human race, as if a saint had just died that very minute, instead of centuries ago. The desperate grieving and lamenting was as real as life. The intonations of the men offering prayers were topped only by the prayers of the hundreds in the adjoining mosque. I became a self-conscious eavesdropper. The din of jumbled voices transferred the hysteria to me. My heart ached for those honest believers who were releasing their bottled up emotions. As I felt their need for this outpouring I wanted to reach out to them in sympathy. I, too, became emotionally overwhelmed. The suffering of all humanity, the hopes, the fears, the failures, the despair, permeated the air undisguised.

I carefully stole a glance at Ali, and in the dim light he appeared as one of the most austere and saintly shadows I had ever seen. He was motionless, except for the tremor of the hand hanging by his side nearest me. This was the first time I had ever known Ali to show any outward sign of uneasiness. His obvious nervousness made me feel suddenly insecure and a strange, haunting sensation overcame me. I tried to occupy my thoughts by studying the interior in detail. The vaulted ceiling as far up as I dared to look was made completely of mosaic mirrors. Directly over the sarcophagus hung a heavy, crystal chandelier. I had a much better opportunity to study the rich carpets under our feet.

In the middle of my musing, Ali said something to the man who was intoning our prayers. The chant stopped abruptly. He handed him some money and fell into the pilgrims' line of march. I followed, and slowly, slowly we went round the casket. Carefully, I watched Ali to see if we were to kiss it as the others were doing. He came close several times, slightly bowed his head, but continued the measured steps. As we left the casket, we came upon hundreds of supplicants offering their noon prayers in the adjoining mosque. After a long hesitation at the doorway, we walked into a spacious, carpeted room which was almost empty, and after looking about, circled the tomb again, and left.

My shoes were placed in front of me. Now came the test. I gripped my *chador* in my teeth, reached down, keeping my hands inside, and got my feet in far enough so that I could walk away.

Somehow I made it across the courtyard with both my shoes still half on my feet. When we reached the shadows of the exit and were alone, I pulled them on securely, then stood for a few minutes leaning against the wall to get a last and studied look of the sweeping courtyard. Not one of the three of us had yet spoken, but I knew that Ali and Hossein were giving me an opportunity to get that last, privileged look.

Once outside, Ali hailed a drosky. As we jolted along, the men talked quietly in Persian; I sat speechless, motionless.

When we came into sight of Sherm and the car, we could see that he was surrounded by children. Sherm was sitting in the back seat looking ahead, pretending

not to see them. His fur hat had evidently created
quite a sensation.

Hastily we got out, and without a word, Ali jumped
into the front seat, followed by Hossein. I could hardly
get the tail end of my *chador* in the back seat as he
sped away.

As soon as we were well out of sight of the children, Ali looked back at us. "Sherm, you shouldn't
have been cracking and eating those pistachio nuts.
You know it is Ramazan. You aren't supposed to eat
in front of fasting people, especially in this town."

"My gosh—forgot all about that. Here I was, trying so hard not to attract attention. I had them way
down in my lap and didn't think anybody could see
them. Those kids had been talking to me ever since
you left, but I had to play deaf and dumb because
I didn't dare answer them."

"Those kids probably noticed you were eating. They
were asking you who you were and where you came
from. Boy, I didn't know I was going to have to worry
about you, too! You know, in the shrine, my knees
got just like—what you call it—jell—jelly, jello——"

"From the bottom of my heart, I now appreciate
what you went through to take me to the shrine.
Honestly, I didn't realize it would be so overpowering.
Ali, when I saw you shaking, of all people, then I knew
there must be something to worry about. However, I
knew nobody would pay any attention to me—I looked
like all the other women in their *chadors*."

"Oh, no you didn't! In the first place you were a
little taller. And anybody could see you didn't know

how to wear it. We were lucky—that's all I can say. I didn't want to frighten you too much, but it was really dangerous—especially during these mourning days. You saw all those hundreds of people. You can imagine what they would do in their emotional state if they found a non-believer in their midst. Wow! I'm exhausted. Sherm, you better drive now we are out of town. I'm too tired."

"Now I realize you both had a lot of courage to take me there. I honestly didn't know it would be the way it was."

"Courage? Don't be silly. I'm just crazy—haven't got good sense. Anyway, I must tell you that when we finished and you put your shoes on you did it just like a villager. That was a good performance. But, the time I got frightened was when we walked past the check stand. Two men got up and started to follow you. They tried to move in between you and Hossein. He pushed one gently aside and stepped close to you so nobody could get in front of him. This you didn't know. All I can say is that I have never been more scared. I kept thinking what could we three do against that mob of hundreds. Now, that it is all over, what do you say? Was it worth it?"

"It was unforgettable and, to me, it was worth it. I had heard about the magnificence of the shrine, but I couldn't have believed it unless I saw it with my own eyes. One thing I keep wondering—what did the man say when he prayed for us?"

"I don't know—all in Arabic. All our prayers are

Arabic. I caught a word now and then, so I know he was praying for us."

"We certainly needed that. Along with your being a son of Mohammed."

BYE — BYE, *KUTCHE*

BREAKING UP HOUSEKEEPING AND LEAVING TEHRAN was hectic in a different way from that Glendale departure two years before.

Because many overseas contract employees, like ourselves, had to be responsible for completely furnishing their homes in Iran, there was always an exchange of household goods with incoming foreigners or resident Iranians who were looking for bargains.

We were luckier than most, thanks to the major's furniture. His kindness had seen us through with but a minimum of additions, but these extras we had to sell. This we chalked up as another one of our new experiences in a foreign post, that of secondhand furniture and appliance dealers. I dreaded having to go through the ordeal. I dislike selling anything. I often locked myself in my room at the ring of the doorbell, hoping Doran would carry on or that Sherm would get home in the nick of time.

Somehow I felt we should give everything away; however, since we had quite a substantial investment in gas ranges, space heaters, and electrical gadgets, this would have been much too costly.

The last few weeks were filled with gay farewell parties, many of which we enjoyed while sitting on packing crates in our finest clothes (because several of our friends were leaving about the same time, and had already sold most of *their* furniture). With neighbors, friends, and buying prospects meandering through our home and staying for visiting and tea, our last two months became a constant open house.

All this went on with a background of building activity in the compound adjoining us, and the chanting of the bricklayers who sang all day long, "Allah give you the power. Call Ali and send it up. Send two by two (or one by one—or half a brick)" with all the variations.

They did throw him a brick, and sometimes two, all the way to the third story, and never once did I see a fumble. Then the main cross street adjoining ours was torn up in preparation for asphalting, adding greatly to the bewilderment of people trying to get to our house. This new maze almost sealed us off from the outside world. All this digging and chopping started about five thirty every morning.

On top of this annoyance, the air was full of a hate campaign from Radio Moscow, harassing Iran with false and vicious propaganda day and night. Between bursts of Persian music, the Russians ranted in Farsi (the language on which they spend more time than any other foreign-language broadcasts, except English). "Foreigners are pouring into Iran like ants and locusts, depriving Iranians of their rights." Attacks on foreigners, as well as the Iranian government, were relentless. These Communist lies so powerfully spread were bound to have an unsettling effect. That old refrain which held over for a long time after the second World War, "Yankee go home," was occasionally hurled at us now, only with a new twist, "Amerikie go home."

Iran's government radio and press refuted these attacks with a boldness unknown in previous years. To charges that Iranian oil is being exploited by outsiders, they urged Moscow, "Liberate the enslaved Rumanian workers from the claws of Soviet soldiers and hand back the oil to the Rumanian nation." When this was interpreted to us, we gave loud cheers for this small, proud nation, standing up to her giant neighbor on the north.

The last three days the usual, unpredictable events occurred. Our hard-headed landlord and wife arrived on our doorstep one evening as Ali was conferring with us about the few remaining things we had yet to sell. It was rather late in the game for the landlord to come around pressing to raise the rent, as he had done for two years, so we were quite mystified as to the reason for his visit. We couldn't believe it when, through Ali, he invited us to celebrate the Passover with him and his family. After his raging and the trouble he caused me signing our lease, I never expected this foe to turn into a friend. We were hesitant to accept, suspecting some ulterior motive, but Ali convinced us that the landlord really liked us since he had come to know us, and wanted very much for us to celebrate with his family!

After we accepted, Ali talked further with him. In his smooth, unassuming manner, Ali gave them a sales story on our butane kitchen stove. We stood by while he described, through extravagant gestures what beautiful *pillo* it would make. He opened the oven and showed what a cinch it would be to make kebab like they had never tasted before. No one could have known less about stoves, kitchens, and housekeeping than Ali, but he had a great imagination. The advantages over kerosene and open fire brought the sale to its final conclusion. This supersalesmanship sold the stove at our asking price. Ali had convinced them right off that bargaining would be out, as we were very sensitive to that sort of thing.

Next, he led them to a bedroom, and before we knew it, and the landlord realized what had happened to him, he had gained two beds, which he probably didn't need. Ali coasted quickly through the house, looking every place, then he whispered to Sherm, "Is that all?"

"That's all," Sherm replied.

Ali walked back into the kitchen as the landlord was inspecting his stove, and there spotted a shiny, white kitchen stool he had not noticed before, so he tried to sell this, too. Sherm attempted to break in, and so did the landlord, but nobody could get a word in until Ali had finished. The landlord finally put over the idea that he already owned the stool. It belonged to him and went with the house.

This error was quickly glossed over. Ali proceeded to sell the wall can opener which we had overlooked. The landlord left that evening with furniture he probably didn't want and might never use.

Then the very next day I became a heroine, at least

in the eyes of Maryam Niami. I had picked her up in our car to take her to lunch, when the car stalled at the most congested intersection of Tehran at the busiest hour of the day. Iranian drivers, as a rule, do not stop for anything, much less stalled cars, and that day was no exception. From all four directions they bore down upon us. Mrs. Niami dropped her head in her lap and began to moan, "How awful! They will run into us and kill us."

"Maybe someone will give us a push," I consoled as I leaned out the window looking helplessly around for assistance. Fortunately, a policeman appeared from somewhere and pushed us to the curb. Now that we were out of the way, we expected the traffic to proceed at its usual accelerated speed. Instead, the lines stopped moving, and the drivers just perched on their seats, ogling expectantly to see what we would do. A few got out of their cars and moved toward us as if to offer help.

I started to get out of the car. "Thank goodness we got out of that tight squeeze alive. Now that we are away from those maniacal drivers, I can fix it."

Mrs. Niami grabbed my skirt and dragged me back in. "All these people are watching! We better hire a taxi driver or someone who knows how to repair it. A woman can't get out in the street and try to fix a car. It would be so terribly embarrassing. They think it is crazy for women to drive anyway—they aren't very used to it yet. Now, if you get out there and try to be a mechanic—oh, please, don't do it."

I managed to slide out and get to the hood. I lifted

it up, and in a second pushed the loose wires back into the distributor. We had been having this car trouble for two days and Sherm had shown me what to do. I hopped back in and, before an audience of about fifteen men who had crowded around us, and the lines of traffic still waiting and watching, I drove away—slowly—so as to get the full benefit of those amazed and incredulous looks.

"Oh," Mrs. Niami sighed loudly, "I am so proud of you. How did you ever do it? Look, see those men —they can't believe a woman could fix a car. Look at them, Maxine dear—just look." She turned around and stared toward the back window and laughed and laughed.

I know absolutely nothing about motors, but I was never able to convince Mrs. Niami of this, and my fame spread all over Tehran.

The evening was also eventful. Our friends, Bunny and Clifford Kamen, from Glendale, had arrived in town. Cliff is the leading travel-film producer and lecturer in the United States and had come to Iran to do "The Splendors of Persia," one of the first travel movies of this little-known country. They had almost despaired of ever getting the tea drinking over with and settling down to business. A large party honoring them was given by a prominent Iranian.

At this party, Ali met another blue-eyed girl. She was the only single girl guest and came with her distinguished father, a general. As soon as I noted her blue eyes (Ali's weakness) and established that she was not married, I maneuvered myself next to her on a love seat. She spoke beautiful English, luckily for me, and we found many friends in common. When I learned she was a cousin of Mrs. Niami, I knew her family was important enough to be acceptable.

Ali eventually ambled by us, and I all but tripped him to get him to stop so I could make the introduction. In presenting her, I put the emphasis on MISS. He got the point and hesitated a moment. Casually, I invited him to sit down and talk with us. He eyed the love seat skeptically, which would be crowded for three, but I thought it would be a *close* opportunity for them to get acquainted. Self-consciously he tried to escape. I was so persistent that if he refused it would have been an affront to me. I moved over so that he had to sink down between the girl and me, and very close to the girl, after a pronounced shove from me.

After they talked awhile in English, they went into Persian, a clever way of eliminating me. I was dying to understand what they were saying, but they lost me completely.

Afterwards, Ali told me that this girl was the one his mutual friends, who had led him to the first Blue Eyes, had been trying to have him meet for months —but he had been too busy. Anyway, he gave me credit for the actual introduction and for squeezing him over close to the girl.

Late afternoon of the next day Ali came by to bring us an up-to-the-last-minute report on the new Blue Eyes. Our host and a woman cousin of Ali's, who was present at the party, had connived to get him to the host's home on some flimsy pretext. As soon as he arrived he was bombarded with over forty pictures of the girl, and given the "standing room only" approach—"Get it now before it is too late."

"I am leaving for Europe in a week," the host had said, "and I would like to have a little engagement party for you and Ezete before I leave."

"Oh, this is too fast," Ali had answered. "I must have time to investigate her family and—well—think it all over. Just at this time I have too many problems, about the villages and other things. I prefer to wait until you come back in four months."

"Impossible! She is so good, she will be gone by then. If you don't snap her up now you will be sorry. There are others, you know, who want her. May be your last chance."

"If she goes there will be another one someplace. I need time."

"Ezete's father is my best friend. Let me go to him tonight and arrange it. Your cousin has discussed this with your mother and she is willing to proceed with an inquiry into her family. You must not delay!"

Ali told us, "I didn't know what to say, everybody pressing me. Maybe she is the right one—I don't know. Anyway, just to get out of that house I told them to give me until the end of the week. How do I know if I like her? They tell me she liked me, but how can she know—only talking with me a few minutes. If I could only take her out on dates, about five times, then I would know for sure, but that is out of the question."

I hated to leave until I knew the outcome of this, but Ali has sworn to keep us informed in detail, by mail and radiogram, if necessary, of the progress of this potential match.

The original one year we intended to live in Iran had stretched to two because of the eagerness and urging of Sherm's Iranian associates that he continue in his work. Also, we had found the country and people absorbingly interesting and felt the second year would give us still better and deeper understanding of their thinking, their problems.

Our adjustment to Iran had been simple, we felt, compared to that of many Iranians who go to the States. This was because of the understanding and help we received from so many new Iranian and American friends when we first arrived. Although we certainly didn't know exactly what to expect, we seemed to have a better conception of the Iranian way of life than they have of ours. One Iranian student friend, who spoke excellent English and was well briefed and prepared for what he thought he would find in the States, gives some idea of his surprise in these excerpts from his first letter after his arrival in America.

It is about a week since my arrival in the U.S. I just expected to see huge buildings, huge factories and industrial installations. But the first thing which impressed me was the general condition of the people.

There is no dust, no dirt and no *jubes* in cities. People enjoy every facility of modern life, but they work, and work as hard as possible. Nobody walks slowly. Nobody has time to look at the oddities around him even if one stands nude or walks head down.

Americans are very careful people, showing not even one per cent of what usually American films tell us.

One odd thing is that lots of American ladies wear hats. They dress incredibly respectfully.

Frankly speaking, I expected to see cheap, naked women everywhere. Now, I don't see skirts even above the knees. Nobody can believe this unless he himself visits the U.S.

On our last day in Iran, Sherm and I disconsolately wandered through our vacant, lonely rooms, then on to the terrace where we stood and admired our lovely garden. Leaving Iran was like departing from a loved one whose future was uncertain. Without audibly expressing it to one another, we knew a large part of our hearts would remain in Iran.

Ali was coming to take us to our plane, at the grand, new Mehrabad airport. It had been ten years in the building and was just recently completed.

The gate bell rang, and for the last time Doran let Ali in. Ali stood there looking at us dejectedly. "Are you ready?" He tried to force himself to say it bravely.

"As ready as we'll ever be, I guess," answered Sherm. "Doran insisted on coming to see that we got off properly even though it makes him a day late starting a job with our friends. Mohammed is standing by to help with the luggage."

Ali just wasn't himself. He kept making circles on the tile floor with his right foot. He avoided looking up. "That's a good thing because you are going to need a lot of help with your luggage. I hate to tell you this—but—well—you won't believe it—but——," then he began to chuckle. This was strange behavior for him—especially at a time like this.

"Well—you don't need to be that happy about our leaving," I finally managed half in earnest, half in jest.

"You don't know—you just don't know what is going on outside. Can you imagine after two years of driving up and down this miserable *kutche* that now— today—when you are leaving—it is completely dug up. They are getting it ready to asphalt."

Ali went on. "They have got—exactly in front of your house so nobody can come in or out in a car. When you step out you will see that the whole center is out of the street and the *jube* is running full force down it. Only pipes, sand, and rocks are along the sides. Be careful not to break your legs trying to walk through to my car."

Doran evidently knew about the ground breaking but hadn't wanted to tell us. He slowly opened the gate so we could see. Sure enough, there was the water gurgling past the front of our door and everything just as Ali had described it.

"No!" I shouted. "Oh—no—I can't believe it— after all this time!" I took a quick look up and down. Even the old camel caravan and the donkey train weren't in sight. They couldn't get down the *kutche* either. And this was the one time I would have taken that donkey driver up on his offer to give me a ride. I could have ridden out in true Iranian workman style.

Mohammed had been waiting at the gate, and when we appeared he called to his wife. She, baby in arms, and little Reza rushed up to us.

Our servants began kissing our hands and crying. They had become a part of our family and we their guardians.

News travels fast on any *kutche* and the neighborhood children, all the servants and their children, congregated around our gate. They were handing us flowers and kissing our hands.

Waving, calling farewells, we picked our way through the debris with the devoted little group following us. Finally, I turned my head away so no one could see the tears that came while those wide-eyed children kept calling the American words we had taught them, "Bye, bye—bye, bye," as far as we could hear.

The Millers received the following radiogram a few months after their return to the United States:

BDD0830 27 PD IN TL== CD TEHERAN VIA RCA 9 100 LT SHERMAN MILLERS
    GLENDALE (CALIF)==
THE MAN WITH SUCH STRONG NERVES HAS COME TO HIS KNEES AND HAS CLOSED THE DOORS OF FREEDOM STOP HE HAS BECOME ANOTHER PRISONER OF LOVE STOP BRIDE TO BE AND I EXTEND THE MILLERS OUR HUMBLE INVITATION TO BE WITH US AT TIME OF WEDDING MAY TENTH STOP HER EYES ARE BROWN
                    ALI

U.S.S.R.
CASPIAN SEA
TURKEY
TABRIZ
RAMSAR
CHALUS
GHAZVIN
KARAJ
QUM
SANINDAJ
HAMADAN
IRAQ
ARAK
KERMANSHAH
BAGHDAD
BASRA
KHORRAMSHAR
ABADAN
PERSIAN
SAUDI ARABIA